The Art

Here, in these discern⬛⬛⬛⬛⬛⬛nal observations by Plutarch on life a⬛⬛⬛⬛⬛⬛e wisdom of a great writer of ancient Gree⬛⬛⬛y translated by a distinguished modern scholar w⬛⬛ also has contributed a thoughtful introduction and commentary on each essay.

While Plutarch's *Lives*—the world's classic accounts of famous men—reflect his political brilliance and sophistication, these selections from his *Moralia* reveal another side of his nature: his concern with the ethics of human relationships. From the daily intimacies of home life come his opinions on love, marriage, fidelity, friendship, and child-rearing. He discusses the power of blood ties, ideal harmony between man and wife, the delights and dangers of passion—all the vital factors in family happiness. To each he brings the illumination of Graeco-Roman thought and tradition, tempered by an enlightened, humanitarian outlook which makes his counsel remarkably meaningful for readers today.

All but unobtainable in English before, these seven essays now appear in this new translation for the first time. Moses Hadas, professor of Greek and Latin at Columbia University, is the author of two widely-hailed histories of classical literature, and has translated and edited many other Greek and Latin works.

Other MENTOR Books of Special Interest

LIFE STORIES OF MEN WHO SHAPED HISTORY from Plutarch's Lives (abridged) *edited by Eduard C. Lindeman*

A distinguished selection taken from the John and William Langhorne translation. (#MD166—50¢)

GREAT DIALOGUES OF PLATO *translated by W. H. D. Rouse*

A new translation of "The Republic" and other dialogues of the great philosopher of ancient Greece. (#MD167—50¢)

GREEK CIVILIZATION AND CHARACTER
edited by Arnold J. Toynbee

A companion volume to the famous historian's *Greek Historical Thought.* Brilliant translations of Hellenic life-history. (#M99—35¢)

THE GREEK WAY TO WESTERN CIVILIZATION
by Edith Hamilton

A noted Greek scholar recreates the golden age of Greece and its achievements in literature, science, philosophy, art and democracy. (#MD32—50¢)

On Love, the Family, and the Good Life

Selected Essays of Plutarch

Translated, with Introduction, by Moses Hadas

A MENTOR BOOK

Published by THE NEW AMERICAN LIBRARY

MENTOR BOOKS *are published by*
The New American Library of World Literature, Inc.
501 Madison Avenue, New York 22, New York

PRINTED IN THE UNITED STATES OF AMERICA

Contents

Introduction   7

Dialogue on Love   11

On Brotherly Love   53

Marriage Counsel   79

Letter of Consolation
   to His Wife Upon the Death
   of Their Infant Daughter   93

The Education of Children   101

Flattery and Friendship   123

Contentment   166

Introduction

PLUTARCH is a comfortable companion and a useful one. We can approach him, as we cannot the towering figures of the classical age, without craning our necks, or shading our eyes. And yet he is their heir, in a continuous and uninterrupted tradition, and not an antiquarian examining museum specimens under alien lenses. But though he is a sympathetic son, not a remote descendant, of the ancients, his temper is more European than classical. In place of the bowelless intellectuality of the classics he exhibits a humanitarianism which borders on sentimentality, and in place of their ruthless originality a consistent regard for the uses of tradition. Almost alone in the canon of Greek writers whom Europe has accepted Plutarch can be called charming, and his charm, combined with his broad and direct knowledge, makes him the most effective intermediary between the Graeco-Roman world and our own.

Unlike the austere classics, again, Plutarch is a personal writer, and in the course of his copious works he tells us of his family and friends and reveals his tastes and interests so fully that we may know him more intimately than we do any other Greek writer. He was born in Chaeronea in Boeotia, not far from Delphi, in the middle of the first century A.D. By the time of his maturity, then, all the poets and philosophers and artists, both Greek and Latin, whom the world has agreed to call classics had done their work. He himself studied at Athens, traveled, and must have been among the best educated men of his time. Very early in life he was entrusted with important diplomatic missions. Like other gifted Greeks he settled in Rome, where he achieved professional and social success; he was even granted honorary consular rank, as we know, significantly, from epigraphical evidence, not from his own writings. And then, apparently, at the height of his success, he deserted the world metropolis for his own provincial town, became market inspector of Chaeronea, priest of Delphi, and teacher to the young men of his neighborhood.

But why should a man who had been courted in the world metropolis retire to an obscure village? Why should a man of consular dignity serve as a town magistrate? Why should a man alive to contemporary philosophic currents become an apologist for an obsolescent cult? Why should a lecturer who had been applauded in Rome devote himself to teaching country bumpkins? All that Plutarch himself explicitly says of his situation is in a delightful sentence at the opening of his Life of Demosthenes: it is a small town indeed that he lives in, but if he moved away it would be even smaller. But the nostalgia which motivated Plutarch, as we can see from his life and works, is more than an attachment to his native place.

It was rather a peculiar way of life that Plutarch wished to practice and promulgate, the way of life we call Hellenism, and his object was to make of Hellenism a cult whose values could not be affected by loss of political sovereignty. He attached himself to Delphi because insofar as Greek tradition possessed a focus that focus was Delphi. He held whatever magistracy was available to him because active participation in public life was a part of Greek tradition. And most important, he discoursed to the youth of philosophy and literature and music and science, because concern with these matters was the sign manifest of Hellenism. The Lives too were written to inculcate loyalty to Hellenism. Their object was not, as has been thought, to introduce Greeks to Romans or Romans to Greeks, but to show Greeks that even their generals and statesmen had equaled or surpassed the Romans; there was no need to advertise Greek poets and philosophers and artists because in these categories the Romans themselves readily acknowledged Greek superiority. The totality of the past, for Plutarch, provides not only the truest example but the highest sanction for civilized and humane conduct in the present, and it was the duty of those who had a special loyalty to Hellenism to spread its values abroad among peoples whose own past was not so privileged but who were yet susceptible to the evangel.

The loyal heir of a tradition can appreciate its totality better than any late-comer can, but he may be unaware of deviations or developments in that tradition which he himself had caused. These, the late-comer, perhaps because his evidence is fragmentary, can apprehend more clearly. What strikes the modern reader who comes to Plutarch by way of Plutarch's own classical antecedents is a new gentleness, softness, philanthropy—qualities which the classics, if they had known the word, might have dismissed as sentimentality, but which to us carry a suggestion of Christian charity. St. Paul had indeed preached in Greece when Plutarch wrote, but Plutarch's humanity is quite independent. There is an unexampled reverence for womanhood, a touching tenderness for little children, a deep sympathy for animal creation, and, so far as such a thing was possible for an aristocratic Platonist, a respect for all the disinherited of the earth. It is his humanitarianism, in large part, which made Plutarch so appealing to Montaigne and to Shakespeare and which makes him so useful to us. He speaks with the highest authority for his own world, and is an ideal interpreter of that world to us because he is also a member of our world.

Plutarch's writings fall into two main divisions: the universally familiar Lives, and an even larger body of miscellaneous treatises called, with only vague or partial appropriateness, Moralia. Some of these treatises are merely collections of sayings—of famous kings, women, Spartans —some are philosophical essays, one fine group is comprised of reasoned and eloquent apologetics for Delphi, and some, probably dating from Plutarch's early youth, are rhetorical display pieces such as every ambitious student produced. Scholars have regarded the latter with a suspicion, sometimes amounting to certainty, that they are spurious.

The pieces in the present collection have been chosen not for their profundity or novelty or literary excellence but for their relevance to a theme which is characteristically Plutarchan. Throughout his writings Plutarch's main preoccupation is with ethics, and the central theme is ethics in personal relationships. His strong feeling for family ties is obvious in all his works, and he clearly had a genius for friendship, which he regards as Nature's surrogate for kinship. The *Dialogue on Love* deals with a basic human relationship and is a good introduction to Plutarch's approach in all his philosophic writings. Dependence on Plato is so obvious that the treatise may well serve as a commentary on the master, but the doctrine is humanized, moralized, and made relevant to problems of ordinary life, Ethical instruction with a strong humanitarian bias is the obvious intention of the essay *On Brotherly Love*. This essay serves as a kind of transition to others which deal with friendship in the larger sense. Plutarch is nearer the modern than the classic in making marriage the closest of human ties, and the *Marriage Counsel* suggests a foundation for amiable domesticity. The moving *Letter of Consolation to His Wife* provides an eloquent illustration of this amiable domesticity in practice. The essay on *The Education of Children* is so rhetorical in expression and so bumptious in tone that many scholars have condemned it as spurious; those who accept it as genuine assign it to Plutarch's youth. With all its obtrusive rhetoric and elaboration of the obvious the treatise is generally consistent with Plutarch's views; its admonitions may still be useful and, in any case, they throw a welcome light on an important aspect of ancient society. Plutarch's fullest and most illuminating examination of a variety of personal relationships is *Flattery and Friendship*, which may serve as a summary of what he says on the subject in other treatises. The goal of all ethical teaching is the attainment of contentment; Plutarch's *Contentment* is almost an epitome of the moral doctrine implicit in much of his writing and is itself a charming as well as edifying essay.

To facilitate reference, the chapter numbers of the original text are given, in parentheses, at the top of each left-hand page.

Dialogue on Love

The *Dialogue on Love* is artistically among the most successful of Plutarch's writings. The setting, the occasion, and the mood are skillfully and attractively sketched, the intriguing love-story comes in naturally and constitutes a perfect text for the discussion, the interlocutors are individualized and their opinions grow naturally out of their personalities. The dialogue form, in other words, is not merely a device to elicit set responses, as in Plato's lesser imitators, but as in Plato himself it enables the reader to witness and share the actual shaping of the argument. In matter as well as form the shadow of Plato, especially in his *Phaedrus* and *Symposium*, looms large over this treatise. But Plutarch's own gentleness and humaner morality shine through. Indeed he would seem to be criticizing the master, for he makes wedded love at least equal to homosexuality, and it is clear that only his profound piety for Plato, whom he always regards as the supreme authority in philosophy, allows him to countenance homosexuality at all.

As often in Plato, the entire dialogue, after the opening paragraph, is an account of a significant conversation of long ago reported, at the solicitation of friends, by someone who has direct knowledge of it. The friends in this case are Flavianus and his unnamed companions, and the narrator is Autobulus, who had got the story from his father Plutarch, who figured largely in the conversation. Some critics have thought that Autobulus himself must be the author of the treatise, but there is no reason to suppose that Plutarch would not use a traditional device for disclaiming direct authorship. The occasion, circumstances, and persons of the conversation are set forth in the opening paragraphs.

F LAVIANUS: You will now consent, Autobulus, to our request for an account of that discussion on Love, whether you have it recorded in writing or fixed in your memory from having repeatedly interrogated your father on the subject. Tell me, was it at Helicon that the discussion took place?

AUTOBULUS: At Helicon, indeed, Flavianus, at the shrine of the Muses, when the Thespians were celebrating the festival of Love. Every four years they hold a magnificent and impressive festival to Love as well as to the Muses.

FLAVIANUS: We have a favor to ask of you, all of us who have come to hear your recital. Do you know what it is?

AUTOBULUS: No, but I shall if you tell me.

FLAVIANUS: Please dispense, in your present discourse, with the meads and bosks of the poets, with twining ivy and smilax, with all the landscape painting which greedy writers wrest from Plato, transcribing with more diligence than grace his pellucid Ilissus and the gentle herbage beckoning from it.

AUTOBULUS: My narrative has no need whatever of such preambles, good Flavianus. The dramatic circumstances out of which the discussion arose want but a chorus and a stage to make a tragedy. We need only pray for the propitious assistance of the Muses' mother [Memory] to make my report a faithful one.

It was long before I was born, when my father had only recently married my mother. Some misunderstanding and bickering had come between their parents, and my father went to Thespiae to offer sacrifice to Love; he took my mother along to the festival, for it was to her that the prayer and offering pertained. He was accompanied by his intimate friends from Chaeronea, and at Thespiae he met Daphnaeus, son of Archidamus (Daphnaeus was in love with Simon's daughter Lysandra, and was the most favored of her suitors), and Soclarus, son of Aristion, who had come from Tithora. There were also present his old acquaintances Protogenes of Tarsus and Zeuxippus the Lacedaemonian. My father said that a good many well-known Boeotians were there also.

They spent two or three days together, I believe, quietly discussing scholarly questions in the palaestras and theaters in the city. Then, to escape a troublesome contest of cithern players which would involve solicitations and partisanships, most of them broke camp, as before the advance of an enemy, and bivouacked at the Muses' shrine on Helicon.

Early in the morning there came to join them Anthemion and Pisias, both reputable gentlemen, and each attached to Bacchon, who was styled "The Fair." The two were at odds with each other, after a fashion, because of rivalry for Bacchon's favor.

The position was this. At Thespiae there lived a lady called Ismenodora, rich and well born, who had led an exemplary life, by Zeus; she had lived as a widow for no small space without reproach, though she was young and made a good appearance. But Bacchon's mother was an intimate friend of hers, and Ismenodora was seeking to arrange a match for him with a girl of suitable family, and so it came about as a result of their frequent meetings and conversations that Ismenodora herself conceived a liking for the young man. She heard and herself made laudatory remarks about him, and she observed that a crowd of distinguished suitors were in love with him, and so she too became enamored of him. Her intentions were not dishonorable; she wished to marry Bacchon openly and spend her life with him. The project itself seemed unusual, and the mother had misgivings about a connection too eminent and proud for her son. Moreover, some of the lads who went hunting with Bacchon deterred him by remarking on the disparity of Ismenodora's age. Their jests were more effective obstacles to the marriage than were the arguments of more serious persons, for he was ashamed being himself only a cadet to marry a widow. Still, Bacchon disregarded his other advisers, and briefed Pisias and Anthemion to direct his course. Anthemion was his cousin, but older; and Pisias was the most serious of his suitors. Pisias therefore opposed the marriage and attacked Anthemion for willingness to sacrifice the young fellow to Ismenodora. Anthemion for his part criticized Pisias' conduct: he was a worthy enough man in other respects, he said, but in depriving his friend of home and wedlock and great wealth he was following the example of base lovers, so that Bacchon might continue to strip before him in the palaestra as long as possible with bloom untouched.

It was to avoid mutual recriminations which might lead to some passionate outbreak that Anthemion and Pisias had approached my father and his companions to serve as referees and arbiters. Of the rest of the company, as if by prearrangement, Daphnaeus played the advocate for Anthemion and Protogenes for Pisias.

Protogenes began by abusing Ismenodora roundly, whereupon Daphnaeus exclaimed: "By Heracles, what is a man to expect if even Protogenes has come to declare war on Love, when all his conduct, playful and serious alike, is aimed at Love and furthered by Love? 'He forgetteth his books; his country he forgetteth.' Is he not like Laius who absented himself from his country no more than a five-days' journey?[1] But Laius' was a slow and landlubberly Love; your Love, Protogenes, 'with wings whirring flies o'er the sea' from Cilicia to Athens, to view the handsome lads and follow their walks." The fact is that something like this was the reason for Protogenes' migration from Tarsus.

There was a burst of laughter, and Protogenes spoke up: "Do you imagine that I am making war on Love? In point of fact I am defending Love against the unbridled wantonness which imposes the fairest and holiest of names upon shameful deeds and passions."

"Do you call marriage and the union of man and wife shameful?" interposed Daphnaeus; "there can be no bond more sacred."

"Such unions are necessary for propagation of the race," said Protogenes, "and so our lawgivers have been careful to endow them with sanctity and exalt them before the populace. But of true Love the women's apartment has no shred. For my own part I deny that the word 'love' can be applied to the sentiment you feel for women and girls, no more than flies can be said to 'love' milk, or bees honey, or victualers and cooks can be said to have amorous feelings for the beeves and fowl they fatten in the dark.

"Nature induces a moderate and sufficient appetite for bread and relish, and excessive appetite which grows into a passion is called gluttony and gourmandizing. Just so

---

[1] Laius, father of Oedipus, went from Thebes to Pisa for love of Pelops' handsome son Chrysippos. Traditionally this was the earliest instance of pederasty in Greece: see Plato, *Laws* 8.836b; Athenaeus 3.602 ff. Euripides' lost *Chrysippos* dealt with the theme.

nature requires the mutual pleasure men and women give one another, but when the impulse becomes so violent and intense as to be excessive and intractable we cannot properly call it Love. A noble love which attaches to a youthful spirit issues in excellence upon the path of friendship. From these desires for women, even if they turn out well, one may enjoy only physical pleasure and the satisfaction of a ripe body. So Aristippus testified when someone charged that Lais did not love him; 'nor do I suppose that wine loves me, or fish,' said he, 'but I take pleasure in the use of both.' The fact is that the end of desire is pleasure and enjoyment. But Love when it has lost the expectation of friendship, is unwilling to persevere; he will not attend upon a bright bloom if it will not yield the fruit appropriate to its character in the way of friendship and excellence.

"You recall what the husband in the tragedy said to his wife: 'Hatest me? Easily do I bear thy hate, for I count my dishonor a gain.' Nothing could be more amorous than a man who endures a troublesome and unloving wife not for the sake of gain but because of venery and carnality. So the comic poet Philippides mocked the orator Stratocles in the line, 'She turns her back on you, and you barely kiss her pate.' If it is proper to call an affection of this kind love, it is an effeminate and bastard love, confined to the women's apartment as it is to Cynosarges.[1] Rather it is like the eagle which they call the 'true' or 'mountain' eagle, which Homer calls the 'black' or the 'hunter,' whereas there are breeds of spurious eagles who catch fish and sluggish birds in marshes, and when they go hungry, as they often do, they give forth a wretched starveling cry. Just so there is only one genuine Love, that of boys. It is not 'shining with desire,' as Anacreon wrote in his 'Maidens' Song,' nor is it 'drenched in myrrh and bedizened.' But you will see that it is unadorned and untitivated, devoted to philosophic discourse or, it may be, haunting the gymnasia and palaestras in its quest, strenuously and nobly urging those worthy of attention to the path of excellence.

"But that other spineless and indoor love which dallies

[1] The only Athenian gymnasium to which bastards and foreigners were admitted.

on the bosoms and beds of women, always pursuing and indulging in soft pleasures which are without manliness, friendship, exaltation, one must reject. So Solon rejected it: to slaves he forbade the love of males and the use of the gymnasium, but he did not prevent them from intercourse with women. Friendship is a noble and cultivated thing; but pleasure is vulgar and illiberal. Hence it is neither liberal nor cultivated to be in love with slave boys; such a love is mere carnality, like the love of women."

Protogenes was eager to continue his speech, but Daphnaeus broke in: "You did well to mention Solon! Let us cite his opinion of a man in love: 'Caress thou the lads in the lovely bloom of their youth, their delectable thighs, their sweet lips.' And to Solon add Aeschylus, who says: 'No regard hast thou for the bright splendor of thy thighs, ingrate, covered with my kisses.' Others may mock the poets who bid lovers examine hams and coccyx as soothsayers inspect sacrificial victims; I myself regard this as a resounding argument in favor of women. If unnatural intercourse with males does not destroy or even injure a lover's affection, it is all the more probable that the love of women or of men in conformity with nature will lead to friendship through complaisance. Complaisance, my dear Protogenes, is what the ancients called the female's acquiescence to the male. So Pindar speaks of Hephaestus as born of Hera 'without complaisance.' To a young girl not yet ripe for marriage Sappho writes, 'To me you seem but a little child, without complaisance.' And to Heracles someone puts the question: 'Did you enforce complaisance, or did you persuade the girl?' But intercourse with unwilling males effected by violence and rape, or even with willing ones who effeminately and dissolutely and unnaturally suffer themselves, as Plato [*Phaedrus* 250e] says, 'to be covered and impregnated' after the fashion of quadrupeds, is complaisance thoroughly uncomplaisant, ugly, and without Aphrodite's charm. I therefore believe that Solon wrote the lines you cited when he was young and, in Plato's words [*Laws* 839b] 'burgeoning with abundant seed.' But when he grew older he wrote these lines: 'Now are the works of the Cyprian goddess dear to me, and of Dionysus and the Muses, which furnish joy to mankind.' It is as if he had emerged from the stormy tempests of the love of boys and had fixed his life in the serenity of matrimony and philosophic calm.

"If we examine the truth of the matter, Protogenes, the passion for boys and for women derives from one and the same Love. But if you insist on distinguishing between them for argument's sake, you will find that the Love of boys does not comport himself decently; he is like a late issue, born unseasonably, illegitimate and shady, who drives out the elder and legitimate Love. It was only yesterday, my friend, or the day before, after lads began to strip and bare themselves for exercise, that it crept surreptitiously into the gymnasia with its allurements and embraces, and then, little by little, when it had fledged its wings full in the palaestras, it could no longer be held in check; now it abuses and befouls that noble conjugal Love which assures immortality to our mortal kind, for by procreation it rekindles our nature when it is extinguished.

"Protogenes denies there is pleasure in the Love of boys: he does so out of shame and fear. He must have some decent pretext for attachment to his young beauties, and so he speaks of friendship and excellence. He covers himself with athlete's dust, takes cold baths, raises his eyebrows, and declares he is chastely philosophizing—to outward view and because of the law. But when night falls and all is quiet then 'sweet is the fruit when the keeper is gone.' If, as Protogenes maintains, intercourse with boys does not partake of venery, how can there be Love with Aphrodite absent? To attend and serve Aphrodite is the role the gods have allotted to Love, and to share in her honor and power insofar as she vouchsafes him to do so. But if there is Love without Aphrodite it is like inebriation without wine, produced by a brew of figs or barley; the turmoil is fruitless and unsatisfying and soon turns to loathing and revulsion."

During these remarks it was plain that Pisias was irritated and in a temper with Daphnaeus. When Daphnaeus paused for a moment Pisias broke in: "By Heracles, what insolence and impudence! Can men confess that they are tied to females by their sexual organs like dogs to bitches? Can they displace and banish the god from gymnasia and cloisters and from pure and open conversations in the sun and shut him up with the brothels and razors and drugs and sorceries of lascivious women? Chaste women have no business at all with loving or being loved."

At this point my father says he took Protogenes by the arm and quoted to him: " 'This word will call the Argive folk to arms.' By Zeus," he added, "Pisias' want of moderation makes us advocates for Daphnaeus. He sees in wedlock an association empty of love and void of friendship, which is a divine gift. If it lack loving suasion and complaisance we should see that wedlock could be maintained only with difficulty by shame and fear, almost as by bridle and bit."

"This argument carries little weight with me," rejoined Pisias. "Daphnaeus I regard as being in the same state as bronze. Bronze is not so easily melted by fire as by other bronze heated to a liquid which is poured over it, whereupon it too is fused into liquid. So it is not the beauty of Lysandra which afflicts him, but his long contact with a man [i.e., Plutarch] who is aflame and filled with fire that has kindled him and filled him with a like fire. If he does not quickly escape to our side it is plain that he will be completely melted down. But I perceive that I am doing just what Anthemion is most eager for me to do—offending the judges. So I will stop."

"A profitable decision," said Anthemion; "it were better if you had spoken to the point from the beginning."

"My position," said Pisias, "is this: I freely proclaim that as far as I am concerned every woman can have a lover, but a young man should be on his guard against a woman's wealth. By mingling him with so much eminence and grandeur we may inadvertently efface him, like tin in bronze. For so young a man it would be an achievement if he could assert himself, like wine in water, in a marriage with a simple and unpretentious woman. But we see that Ismenodora intends to dominate and control; else she would not reject suitors of high position, birth, and wealth

herself to woo a stripling who still wears the cadet's cape
and needs a tutor.

"It is for this reason that sensible husbands are careful
to cut down their wives' excessive wealth, like clipping a
bird's wings; for it is wealth which makes them lickerish
and frivolous and inconstant and vain, and often enough
they soar up and fly away. And even if they bide at home
it is better for a man to be chained by fetters of gold, such
as they use in Ethiopia, than by his wife's riches."

"One point you miss," subjoined Protogenes, "and that
is that we risk perpetrating an absurd and ridiculous re-
versal of the injunction of Hesiod, who says [*Works and
Days* 696 ff.]:

> Take to thy home a woman for thy bride
> When in the ripeness of thy manhood's pride:
> Thrice ten thy sum of years, the nuptial prime;
> Nor fall far short, nor far exceed the time.
> Four years the ripening virgin should consume,
> And wed the fifth of her expanded bloom.

But it is to a woman as many years older that we are about
to graft this green and immature husband, like men who
speed the ripening of dates and figs.

" 'Oh, but she is in love with him, and all on fire.' Who is
to prevent her from besieging his door, from singing the
serenade of the excluded lover, from decking his pictures
with garlands, from outdoing her rivals in physical prowess? This is standard practice for lovers. And let her relax
her arched brows and put an end to her indulgence and
adopt the posture suitable to such a passion.

"But if she is shamefaced and sober, let her sit at home
and wait for suitors and wooers. A man ought to avoid
and abominate a woman who declares her love; he ought
not undertake marriage with her under the impression that
such lasciviousness is a valid motive."

When Protogenes had concluded, my father spoke. "Do
you see, my dear Anthemion," he said, "they still make
common cause against us and compel us to argue for conjugal Love, when we do not deny or evade the imputation
of serving as his chorus."

" 'Tis so, by Zeus," said Anthemion. "Do defend Love against them more fully. Marshal your forces in support of wealth also, for that is the particular bugaboo Pisias is trying to scare us with."

"What might not be made a reproach to a woman," said my father, "if we reject Ismenodora because she is in love and rich? She is indeed proud and rich. What if she is beautiful and young? What if she is of proud and illustrious birth? Do not prudish ladies have a hateful and intolerable character because of their severity and crabbedness? Do not people call them Furies because their prudishness makes them always irascible with their husbands? Might it not be better to cohabit with some Thracian Habrotonon or some Milesian Bacchis without solemnities, fetched from the market for a price and welcomed [like a new-bought slave] with a shower of nuts? But we know of not a few men who served in durance vile even to such women. Flute girls and Samian dancers, an Aristonica, an Oeanthe with her tambourine, an Agathoclea have trampled upon the diadems of kings. The Syrian Semiramis was chambermaid and concubine to a homeborn slave of King Ninus. The great King Ninus happened upon her and fell in love with her, and she so dominated and despised him that she asked him to permit her to sit upon the throne one day, wearing the diadem, and to direct affairs of state. He consented and gave orders that the same service and obedience be given her as had been given to himself. At first she made but moderate use of her authority, to make trial of the guards. But when she observed that they obeyed her without question or hesitation she ordered them to seize Ninus, then to fetter him, and finally to kill him; and when these orders were executed she ruled brilliantly over Asia for many years. And Belestiche, by Zeus—was she not a barbarian female bought in the market, and do not the Alexandrians have shrines and temples bearing the king's inscription 'To Aphrodite—Belestiche because of his love of her'? And she who shares temple and rites with Love in this city, [Phryne] whose gilt statue stands with those of kings and queens at Delphi—what dowry had she to dominate her lovers?

"But just as these men unwittingly fell a prey to women

because of their own softness and want of strength, so, on the other hand, many men poor and unknown to fame who have married rich and elegant ladies have not been corrupted nor yielded a whit of their spirit but have lived their lives out respected by their wives and governing them with benevolence. But a man who shrinks his wife down and reduces her to small size, as a man does with a ring too big for fear it may slip from his finger, is like those who dock and clip their mares and then take them to a river or pond; it is said that when the mares see their shorn and disfigured reflection they give up their proud neighing and submit to copulation with asses.

"To choose a woman's wealth above virtue or family is vulgar and base, but to avoid wealth when it is joined to virtue and family is foolish. Antigonus wrote to his commander who was fortifying Munychia and ordered him not only to make the collar strong but to make the dog lean —intimating that he should reduce the Athenians' resources. But there is no need for the husband of a rich or beautiful woman to make his wife ugly or poor. Rather by self-control and prudence and by not being overwhelmed by her advantages he should maintain his equilibrium and his dignity, adding the weight of his character, as it were, to his side of the scales, whereby his wife is governed and managed justly and at the same time profitably.

"As for the time of life appropriate for marriage, Ismenodora is of suitable age to bear children and Bacchon to beget them. I understand that the lady is in her prime. And," he added with a smile at Pisias, "she is not older than any of her rivals, nor is she hoaryheaded like some of those who chase after Bacchon! If those people are not too old to consort with him, what is to prevent her from cherishing the young man more than any young girl could do? Young folk are difficult to blend and weld together, and only after a long while and with difficulty do they lay aside their petulance and pride; in the beginning there is stormy weather and resistance to the yoke, especially if Love is involved. Love confounds and overwhelms the marriage, like a gale when there is no pilot, and they are neither able to rule nor willing to be ruled.

"His nurse governs an infant, his teacher the schoolboy, his trainer the cadet, his lover the stripling, and when he comes of age the law and the magistrates govern him; no season of life is without governance and wholly sovereign: why then is it such a frightful thing for an intelligent older woman to pilot the life of a young husband? She would be useful to him by reason of her maturer prudence and sweet and tender by reason of her love. After all," he concluded, "we are Boeotians, and ought to revere Heracles and not take disparity of age in marriage amiss. We know that Heracles gave his own wife Megara in marriage to his son, he being sixteen years old at the time and she three and thirty."

Such was the course of their discussion when, as my father tells the tale, a comrade of Pisias came riding up to them from the city at a gallop, bringing news of an astonishing and bold deed. Ismenodora, it appears, was convinced that Bacchon himself was quite favorably inclined to the marriage and only embarrassed by those who sought to deter him, and so she resolved not to let go of the young man. She therefore summoned those of her male friends who were youthful in their ways and eager to promote her affair and also the most intimate of her woman friends. By prearrangement with them she awaited the hour at which Bacchon customarily left the palaestra and passed by her house, always comporting himself decently. On this occasion, as he came forth anointed after his exercise with two or three of his comrades, Ismenodora herself accosted him at her door, and only touched his smock; thereupon her friends swathed the handsome youth in his smock and cape, carried him into the house in a troop, and immediately shut the door tight. At the same time the women inside pulled his smock off and threw a wedding garment over him. Scurrying servants garlanded the doors with wreaths of olive and laurel, not only Ismenodora's but Bacchon's also. Moreover a flute girl marched through the quarter, piping as she went. Many of the Thespiaeans and the visitors to the city were amused at this escapade, but many others were indignant and urged the gymnasium masters to take steps. These officials, you must know, exercise strict control over the cadets and pay vigilant attention to their conduct. No one now took any thought for the festival contests; all forsook the theater and clustered at Ismenodora's door, discussing the event and debating with one another.

This then was the report brought by Pisias' friend, who had come galloping as if from a battle; he shouted, in great excitement, that Ismenodora had ravished Bacchon. At this, says my father, Zeuxippus laughed and, like the Euripides lover he was, recited the line: "Thy wealth, lady, makes thee proud; but thy thoughts are all too human." But Pisias sprang up and shouted, "Ye gods, where will this license which is subverting our city end? Headstrong liberty is leading straight to lawlessness. But perhaps indignation about laws and rights has become ludicrous, now that the laws of nature are set at nought by a woman's caprice. Did Lemnos itself, [the hearth of female criminality] ever see such a thing? Up," said he, "up and let us hand the gymnasium over to the women, and the senate house too, if our city has wholly lost its sinews!" And so Pisias flung off, and Protogenes accompanied him, partly because he shared his indignation and partly to calm him down.

Anthemion then spoke up: "It was a thoughtless piece of brazenness and truly Lemnian, between ourselves, the act of a woman mightily in love."

"Do you suppose it was really a case of ravishment by force?" rejoined Soclarus with a smile. "Was it not rather a stratagem devised by a sensible young man to escape the embraces of his male lovers by deserting to the arms of a beautiful and rich woman?"

"Never say such a thing, Soclarus," said Anthemion, "never entertain such a suspicion of Bacchon. Even if he were not naturally of a straightforward and open temper he would never have concealed his intentions from me. He shared all his secrets with me, and in this case he knew that I was a warm ally of Ismenodora's. It is love which is 'difficult to fight against' and not, as Heraclitus says, 'anger.' 'Whatever it desireth it purchaseth at the hazard of life'—and of money and reputation. For where can our city show a more decent woman than Ismenodora? When has any shameful tale been bruited about her, or any suspicion of base conduct touched her house? But it does seem that some divine impulse has indeed seized hold of the woman, something stronger than human calculation."

Pemptides remarked with a smile: "It is true there is a disease of the body men call 'sacred.' We need not find it strange, then, if some people call the most raging and ardent passion of the mind 'sacred' and 'divine.' In Egypt I once saw two neighbors disputing as a snake slithered ahead of them on the road. Both considered the serpent a good genius but each insisted that it was his own. Similarly I observe some of you dragging Love into the men's quarters and some to the women's, as being a transcendent and divine good; and so I do not wonder that this passion possesses such great power and esteem that the very people who have reason to drive it out from every cranny and ward it off magnify and exalt it. Hitherto I have held my peace, for I considered that the quarrel pertained rather to private than to public concerns. But now that Pisias is gone I should be very glad to learn from you what the ancients who first declared Love to be a god had in mind."

When Pemptides had concluded and my father had begun to address himself to the subject, another messenger arrived from the city, sent by Ismenodora to fetch Anthemion. The turmoil had grown and there was a difference of opinion among the masters of the gymnasium, one maintaining that they should demand that Bacchon be restored, and the other refusing to meddle in the affair. And so Anthemion rose and departed.

Now my father addressed Pemptides by name. "It is a great and dangerous question that you have laid hold of, Pemptides," he said. "Rather, as I think, you have touched what is wholly untouchable in demanding a detailed explanation and demonstration of the beliefs we hold concerning the gods. Our ancient ancestral faith is sufficient; it is not possible to express or devise clearer proof, a common foundation and basis for piety, and if its solidity and credit is shaken in a single point the whole totters and becomes suspect.

"You must have heard what a clamor was raised against Euripides when he began his *Melanippe* with the line: 'Zeus—whoever Zeus may be; I do not know except by report.' When he was permitted a second attempt (it seems that he had full confidence in the play because it was written with great elegance and care), he changed the line to its present form: 'Zeus, so-called from truth.' Actually, is there any difference between Zeus and Athena or Love in the matter of questioning or even obscuring belief in them by argument and disputation? It is not that Love is only now entering a claim for altar and sacrifice; he is not an upstart sprung from some barbarian superstition, like the so-called Attises and Adonises who have crept in surreptitiously through women and effeminates, to pluck honors to which he had no right; such an upstart should face a charge of usurpation and illegitimacy among the gods.

"It is to Love, my friend [not merely Friendship], that you should suppose the familiar lines of Empedocles to refer: 'Foursquare Friendship, equal in breadth and length, thou perceivest in thy mind, thine eyes may not descry him.' The god is not visible to our eyes, but he is to be believed in along with the most ancient of our deities. And if you demand proof of the existence of each of them, scrutinizing every shrine and subjecting every altar to intellectual tests, you will leave none of them free of allegations and inquisitions. I need go no further than these verses [of Euripides]: 'Seest not how mighty a goddess is Aphrodite? 'Tis she who doth grant and implant love, whose offspring are all we on earth.' Empedocles calls her 'the life-giver,' and Sophocles 'the fruitful one'—both very apt and appropriate designations. This great and admirable function is Aphrodite's; it is but incidental to Love, when he attends upon Aphrodite. But if he is not present then the thing is left wholly without charm and [in Aeschylus' expression] 'unhonored and unfriended.' Intercourse without Love is like hunger and thirst; it is satiated, but beyond this issues in nothing that is fine. But with Love in attendance the goddess banishes satiety of pleasure and produces affection and true fusion. Hence Parmenides declares that Love is the eldest of the works of Aphrodite; in his *Cosmogony* he writes: 'Love she brought forth foremost of all the gods.' Hesiod's approach seems to me more scientific: he made Love the earliest creation of all, so that through him all things might share in creation.

"Therefore if we deprive Love of the observances traditionally paid to him, neither will those which pertain to Aphrodite retain their currency. It is not possible to maintain that one may heap abuse upon Love without insulting Aphrodite, for in the same theater we hear first: 'Love is idleness, and concerns the idle,' and then 'Cypris [Aphrodite], my lads, is not only Cypris but can bear many names: she is hell, she is life imperishable, she is the Fury of madness.' Similarly scarcely one of the other gods has escaped ignorance's readiness to slander and emerged without insult. Consider Ares: his position is pendant to that of Love, as on a bronze relief map, and men have assigned him very high honors; and yet he too has been vilified, as in the lines: 'Blind is Ares, dear ladies; he sees naught, but with his pig's snout roots up all that is evil.' Homer calls him 'murderous' and 'vacillating.' Chrysippus' etymology of the god's name amounts to a slanderous denigration. He said that *Ares* was derived from *anairein* ('to kill'), thus giving occasion to those who believe that the pugnacious and quarrelsome and passionate element in us should be called Ares. Still others hold that Aphrodite is desire, Hermes deft speech, the Muses the arts, and Athena sagacity. You see then what an abyss of godlessness awaits us if we assign our passions, powers, and excellences to the several gods."

"I do see," said Pemptides, "but if it is impious to identify our gods with passions, it is also impious to believe that our passions are gods."

"What do you believe?" asked my father. "Is Ares a god or a passion of ours?" Pemptides replied that he thought Ares was the god who ordered the spirited and virile element in us. Thereupon my father cried out: "Does the pugnacious and warlike and contentious element in us have a god, and the loving and communal and conciliatory element have no god? Is it possible that men who kill and are killed, armor and projectiles and siegeworks and plundering, have as a god, Ares Enyalius or Ares Stratius, as overseer and referee, and that none of the gods serves as witness or overseer or guide or helper when we desire marriage and affection which produces harmony and true partnership?

"Those who hunt antelope and hare and deer have Artemis of the Chase to urge them on and scour after the game with them, and those who snare wolves and bears with pits and nets pray to Aristaeus 'who first devised gins for beasts.' And Heracles, when he was about to draw his lethal bow against the bird, prayed, as Aeschylus says, to another god: 'Hunter Apollo, make thou straight my arrow's flight.' And can it be that for a man who undertakes to capture friendship, the fairest game of all, there is no god or daimon to direct him and share in his effort?

"As for me, my dear Daphnaeus, I cannot think that man is a stock less fair or a shoot less worthy than oak or mulberry or the vine on which Homer bestowed so fine an epithet, for man too possesses a season of burgeoning, which exhibits twofold beauty, of body and also of soul."

"Who in the name of heaven would say otherwise?" interposed Daphnaeus.

"All those, by Zeus," answered my father, "who believe that the care of plowing and sowing and planting is appropriate to the gods (do they not acknowledge certain Nymphs called Dryads, of whom Pindar says that 'the span of their lot is as that of the tree?' and does that poet not also speak of 'Kindly Dionysus who causes the vines to burgeon, autumn's pure rays'?), whereas the nurture and growth of striplings and boys in their season of bloom, when they are molded and fashioned to harmony, is under the care of no god or daimon. They would have it that there is no god to take care that the sprout of man should grow straight in the direction of excellence and that the noble stock should not be bent aside or crushed for want of a guardian or by the wickedness of those it encounters.

"To say such a thing is surely very wrong and ungrateful when at every point we enjoy the benevolence of the divine which spreads over us and nowhere forsakes us in our needs, though the purpose of some of the needs is rather in the nature of necessity than of beauty. The instant of our birth, for example, is not a seemly thing, because of travail and bloody fluxes, and yet there is deity to oversee it, Eileithyia and Locheia. Better it were, indeed, never to have been born than to be born evil for lack of a good protector and patron. Not even when man is sick does deity forsake him: this charge and power is assigned to the god [Asclepius]. Nor even when he dies: there is the god [Hermes] who escorts him from here to there, the champion of the defunct, who puts them to rest and guides their souls, as the poet has him say: 'Night bare me not as master of the lyre nor yet as prophet or healer, but as guide for souls.' All of these functions involve much that is disagreeable; but we can name no task more holy, no competition or contest more seemly for a god to oversee and referee, than lovers' tendance and pursuit of youthful beauties. Here there is nothing of ugliness or necessity but suasion and grace which make for 'sweet toil, labor unlaborious,' and which lead to excellence and friendship. It is 'not without a god' that it achieves its appropriate end, nor does it have any god as guide and master other than Love, companion of the Muses, of the Graces, and of Aphrodite. 'Sweet foison of yearning he soweth in the heart of man,' as Melanippides says; he commingles what is sweetest with what is fairest. Or, my dear Zeuxippus," he concluded, "should we take a different line?"

"I agree, by Zeus," said Zeuxippus, "completely. The contrary opinion is patently absurd."

"How could it be anything but absurd?" said my father. "According to the classification of the ancients there are four species of friendship: first, natural relationship, next the bond of host and guest, third companionship, and finally love. Each of the first three has a patron deity—a god of friendship, or of host and guest, or of kin and clan. Is it not absurd for love alone to be dismissed without a god and patron, like something profane, when in fact it has the greatest need of care and guidance?"

"Yes," said Zeuxippus, "that is entirely illogical."

"In this connection," said my father, "our discourse might well digress somewhat to take cognizance of Plato's position. There is a kind of madness, he says, which is communicated to the soul by the body, and by reason of disharmonious tempers or the intermingling of a noxious circumambient vapor it is rasping and unwholesome and infectious. There is another madness, which is not without divine impulse nor is it self-generated; it is an inspiration from without which disorders our calculation and reasoning, deriving its impulse and energy from a superior power. This passion is commonly called 'enthusiasm,' on the analogy of similar compounds, such as one who is filled with spirit [*pneuma*] is called inspirited [*empnoun*], and one who possesses good sense [*phronesis*] is sensible [*emphron*]; just so agitation of spirit of this sort is named enthusiasm because it shares and participates in a divine [*theos*] power.

"Enthusiasm is of several species. The prophetic sort derives from the inspiration and possession of Apollo, the Bacchic sort from Dionysus: 'With the Corybants dance ye in choir,' says Sophocles; the revels of the Mother Goddess and of Pan are related to Bacchic orgies. The third sort of enthusiasm derives from the Muses and renders the soul tender and chaste; it arouses and excites the poetic and musical element. As for the enthusiasm called battle frenzy or warlike spirit, it is plain to everyone what god arouses it and stirs it up: 'Ares she calleth to arms, stranger to the dance and to the zither, begetter of tears and intestine battle cry' [Aeschylus, *Suppliants* 681 ff.].

"There remains yet one other species of alienation and subversion of the human spirit, Daphnaeus, and it is neither unobtrusive nor noiseless. It is of this species that I should like to ask Pemptides here 'Who of the gods is it that brandishes this thyrsus of fair foliage'—I mean, that amorous enthusiasm for noble youths and chaste women which is the keenest and most fervent enthusiasm of all? As you can readily see, the soldier grounds his arms and gives over his warlike frenzy, 'whereupon his squires gladly strip the armor from off his shoulders' [*Iliad* 7. 121], and

he sits him calmly down to be a spectator of the rest.
Similarly the wild Bacchic and Corybantic bounding
changes and tempers its rhythm and mode from the
trochaic and Phrygian and then ceases. Likewise the
Pythian priestess descends from her tripod and intoxica-
tion of spirit and subsides into calm and quiet. But the
erotic madness which literally possesses men and sets
them aflame neither the Muse of any art nor any 'assuaging
charm' nor change of scene can quench. In the presence of
their beloved they are filled with desire, in his absence they
yearn for him; by day they pursue him and by night bivouac
at his door; when they are sober they invoke the fair
beloved, and when they are drunk they sing of him.

"By reason of their vividness the poet's fancies, it has
been said, are dreams of men awake. Rather should the
expression be applied to lovers, who converse with the object of their love, caress him, and reproach him—all in
his absence! Other fantasies are like figures drawn in
water; they blur quickly and slip from our mind. But the
images of the beloved abide like pictures etched in encaus-
tic and fixed with flame; they remain vivid permanently,
moving, living, speaking. Hence the Roman Cato used to
say that the soul of the lover dwelt in the soul of the
beloved. I should add that the whole soul of the beloved
belongs to the lover—his form, his character, his behavior,
his actions. Drawn by these the lover quickly compasses
a long journey, as the Cynics say, 'a path to virtue at
once direct and short has been discovered.' For so the soul
proceeds by the quickest route to friendship and excellence,
borne, as it were, upon the waves of passion with the god
in attendance. In short, I affirm that the enthusiasm of
lovers is divinely directed and that its patron and pilot is
that very god whose festival we are celebrating and to
whom we are offering sacrifice.

"The gods we classify mainly according to their power
and utility, and as among human values there are two,
sovereignty and excellence, which we regard and designate
as divine. It now devolves upon us to examine, in the first
place, whether Love is inferior to any of the gods in

power. 'Great and mighty is the victory which the Cyprian queen ever bears away,' as Sophocles [*Trachinian Women* 497] says, and great too is the might of Ares. The power of the other gods is divided, in a certain point of view, between these two. The one is closely allied to whatever is beautiful, the other opposed to whatever is ugly; and both are innate in our souls from the beginning. So Plato too distinguishes these forms.

"We must observe at once that the function of Aphrodite, if Love be not present, is to be purchased for a drachma; no one, unless he be in love, undergoes toil or danger for the sake of venery. Not to mention [our townswoman] Phryne in this connection, a Lais, my friend, or a Gnathaenium 'kindles the beam of her lamp at eventide' to invite passers-by, and though she calls to them they ignore her. 'But suddenly the hurricane blast sweeps down' [*Iliad* 17.57] bearing with it great love and desire and raises this same service to the value of the fabled treasures of Tantalus and his realm. So weak and so cloying is the complaisance of Aphrodite without Love's inspiration.

"You may understand this better from what follows. Many men have shared their venery with others, prostituting not only their mistresses but even their wives. That was the case, my friend, of the Roman Gabba. He was entertaining Maecenas, it seems, and when he noticed that Maecenas was nodding and winking to his wife, he quietly turned his head aside and pretended to be asleep. Meanwhile a slave crept into the dining room and was about to make off with the wine, whereupon Gabba glared at him and said, 'Rascal, don't you know that it's only for Maecenas that I am asleep?' But perhaps this is not to be taken seriously for Gabba was a buffoon. But at Argos there were two politicians who were rivals, Nicostratus and Phayllus. Once when King Philip was sojourning in the city Phayllus conceived the idea that if his wife, who was very handsome, would consort with Philip he would obtain some important political appointment. Nicostratus' party got wind of this and picketed Phayllus' house.

Phayllus put high boots on his wife, clothed her with a
cadet's cape and a Macedonian hat to make her look like
a royal page, and so spirited her out of the house.

"But of the numberless lovers of boys that are and have
been do you know of one who prostituted his beloved even
to obtain the honors of Zeus? I do not believe there have
been any. How could there be when men who would not
speak against a tyrant or oppose his policy have in many
cases disputed with tyrants and opposed them when the
favors of their fair boy-lovers was the issue? You surely
know that Aristogiton of Athens and Antileon of Meta-
pontus and Melanippus of Acragas never took issue with
the tyrants of those cities although they saw them waste
the state and behave like men drunk; but when the tyrants
made attempts upon their boy-loves then they defended
them like inviolable and untouchable sanctuaries and took
no heed of their own safety.

"It is told of Alexander that he wrote to Theodorus,
brother of Proteus: 'Send me that music girl and accept
ten talents, that is, unless you are in love with her.' Another of Alexander's companions, Antipatrides, once came
to a banquet with a lutenist, and Alexander was amorously
inclined to the girl. He asked Antipatrides, 'You don't happen to be in love with her?' When Antipatrides answered
that he was very much in love with her, Alexander said,
'A thousand plagues on you!'—but he refrained himself
and did not lay a finger on the woman.

"And now consider the works of Ares," continued my
father, "and see how far superior is Love. He is not
'shiftless,' as Euripides charges, nor unwarlike, nor does
he 'keep vigil on the soft cheek of a maiden' [Sophocles,
Antigone 784]. A man filled full of Love has no need of
Ares to fight his enemies, but knowing that he has his
god within him 'ready is he to venture through fire and
the sea and the blasts of ether' for the sake of his friend,
whatever he may bid him do. Each of the Niobids, in
Sophocles' play named for them, as he was smitten and at
the point of death called on no other ally or helper than
his lover—'Ah, enfold me in thine arms!' You surely

know the story of Cleomachus the Pharsalian and the circumstances of his death in combat."

"We do not," said those of Pemptides' party, "but we would very willingly hear it."

"It is worth hearing," said my father. "Cleomachus had come to aid the Chalcidians when their Lelantine War against the Eretrians was at its height. The Chalcidians thought their infantry was rugged, but it was a difficult thing to counter the enemy's cavalry. His allies therefore invited Cleomachus, a man of magnificent spirit, to make the first sally against the cavalry. Cleomachus asked his beloved, who was present, whether he would be a spectator of the battle. The lad said he would, and kissed him affectionately, and put his helmet on his head. Cleomachus, filled with exultation, gathered the flower of the Thessalians about him, charged brilliantly, and fell upon the enemy with such force as to confound and rout their cavalry. Thereupon the heavy infantry also turned in flight, and the Chalcidians won a complete victory. It befell that Cleomachus was killed; the Chalcidians show his grave in their market place, and a tall pillar stands over it to this day. And whereas they had previously regarded pederasty as an abomination, they then favored it and honored it more than other people. (Aristotle's version is that Cleomachus was indeed killed when he had overcome the Eretrians in battle, but that the man who was kissed by his beloved was one of the Chalcidians from Thrace who had been sent to support the Chalcidians in Euboea. This is the occasion of the ballad which the Chalcidians sing: 'Ye lads endowed with graces and noble fathers, begrudge not enjoyment of your bloom to valiant warriors, for Love which relaxes limbs flourishes along with manliness in the cities of the Chalcidians.' The lover's name was Anton and his beloved's Philistus, as the poet Dionysius records in his *Origins*.)

"Among you Thebans, Pemptides, is it not customary for a lover to present his beloved with a full suit of armor when he comes of age? The battle order for heavy infantry was quite altered and rearranged by Pammenes, who was expert in matters of love. He found fault with Homer as ignorant of love because he trooped the Achaeans by tribes and clans, and did not post beloved by the side of lover, to make 'spear touch spear and helmet helmet' [*Iliad* 13.131]. Of all generals, said he, Love alone is invincible. For men may desert their fellow-tribesmen and kinsmen and even, by Zeus, their parents and children, but never at all has enemy forced apart or come between any inspired lover and his beloved. Even where there is no need they are eager to display their love of danger and contempt of life. Thus Theron the Thessalian clapped his left hand to the wall and then drawing his sword struck off his thumb, challenging his rival in love to do likewise. Another man who had fallen upon his face in a battle asked the enemy who was about to strike him to wait a moment, so that his beloved might not find him wounded in the back.

"Not only are the most warlike of peoples most addicted to boy-lovers, but so also are the heroes of old—Meleager, Achilles, Aristomenes, Cimon, Epaminondas. The last named had two boy-loves, Asopichus and Caphisodorus. Caphisodorus was killed along with Epaminondas at Mantinea and is buried at his side. As for Asopichus, he proved a fearsome warrior and a terror to the enemy, and the first of them that stood up to him and struck him, Eucnamus of Amphissa, had a hero's honors paid him by the Phocians.

"To enumerate all of Heracles' loves is too long a task. But Iolaus, for example, is said to have become his beloved, and to this day lovers honor and revere Iolaus and receive oaths and pledges from those they love at his tomb. Heracles is also said to have saved Alcestis whose life was despaired of (he was something of a physician) as a favor to Admetus, for though Admetus loved his wife, Heracles loved Admetus. According to the myth Apollo too was a lover of Admetus and 'did Admetus service for a long year.'

"It is a good thing that Alcestis has come to mind. Women have nothing to do with Ares, but Love when it possesses them drives them to boldness beyond their nature and even to death. If myths are of any use as evi-

dence, the stories of Alcestis, Protesilaus, and Orpheus'
Eurydice prove that the only god whose orders Hades
heeds is Love. For all the others, as Sophocles says,
'Hades knoweth nor kindliness nor favor; only justice unqualified doth he embrace.' But lovers he does respect,
and to them alone he is neither adamant nor inexorable.
And so it is a good thing, my friend, to share in the initiation at Eleusis, for in my judgment those who have
been initiated into the rites and mysteries of Love enjoy
a better lot in Hades. I do not believe in the myths, nor
yet wholly distrust them. They say good things, and by
some divine chance they touch upon the truth when they
say that there is a path upward for lovers from Hades
to the light of day. Where and how this ascent may take
place they do not know, for they have missed the true
path which Plato first of men perceived through his philosophy. And yet fine rubbings and mists of the truth are
to be found scattered in the mythology of the Egyptians;
but these require a skillful tracker, who is able to seize
upon a great quarry from slight traces.

"We shall therefore leave these things aside, and having
observed the very great strength of Love, let us now examine his benevolence and grace towards mankind. I do not
mean whether Love works good effects for the beloved
(these are perfectly manifest to everyone), but whether
he produces more and greater advantages to the lovers
themselves. Euripides, for example, though he was well
versed in love, marvels at the least of its benefits when
he says: 'It is Love that teaches the poet his art, though
he had been Muse-less before.' The truth is that Love
makes a man acute, though he had been a dullard before
—and, as we have remarked, courageous when he had
been timorous, just as men make soft wood tough by passing it through fire. Every lover becomes generous and
straightforward and magnanimous though he were miserly
before; his pettiness and avarice are relaxed, like iron in
fire, so that he now takes greater pleasure in bestowing
presents upon his beloved than in himself receiving presents from others.

"You surely know the story of Anytus son of Anthe-

mion, who was in love with Alcibiades. Anytus was giving
a sumptuous and elegant entertainment to some friends,
when Alcibiades broke in riotously, seized half of the cups
from the table, and went off. The guests were indignant
and said, 'That young fellow has treated you with outrageous insolence.' 'Nay, rather humanely,' said Anytus,
'for though he might have taken all he has left me these.' "

Zeuxippus was overjoyed. "By Heracles!" said he, "you
have almost banished my inherited hatred of Anytus for
his persecution of Socrates and philosophy if he behaved
so mildly and generously in his love."

"So be it," said my father. "Does not Love make morose
people who scowl at their associates more humane and
agreeable? 'When the hearth burns bright a house is
cheerier to see,' and similarly, it seems, a man is made
brighter by the warmth of love. But the majority of men
behave paradoxically. When they see a beam of light
shining in a house at night they consider it a divine thing
and marvel at it; but when they see a petty and lowly and
ignoble soul suddenly filled full of understanding, liberality, courtesy, grace, generosity, they do not feel constrained to say, with Telemachus, 'Verily, some god is
within' [*Odyssey* 19.40].

"And by the Graces, Daphnaeus," he continued, "here
is surely a most extraordinary thing. The lover despises
virtually everything, not only his companions and kin but
also laws and magistrates and kings; he fears nothing, is
astonished at nothing, is concerned for nothing; is able to
abide 'barbed lightning' [Pindar, *Pythians* 1.5]; and yet
as soon as he beholds his boy-love 'Like a beaten cock
with wings lowered he is confounded,' his boldness is
shattered and his lofty pride crushed.

"It is proper to mention Sappho along with the Muses.
Of Hephaestus' son Cacus the Romans record that he
belched fire and flame out of his mouth; but Sappho
uttered words truly mingled with fire and through her
lyrics sent forth the burning ardor of her heart, 'seeking
to heal her love with the tuneful Muses,' as Philoxenus
says. If Lysandra, my dear Daphnaeus, has not banished
your old habits from your memory, recall to us those

verses in which beautiful Sappho says that upon the appearance of her beloved her voice fell mute, her body burned, she turned pale, and was seized with trembling and dizziness." Daphnaeus recited the familiar lines, whereupon my father added, "Is not this, by Zeus, a manifest divine seizure? Is this not a demonic agitation? Is the Pythian priestess so transported when she lays hold of the tripod? Do their pipes and tambourines so transform the orgiastic worshippers of the Mother of the Gods? Many people see the same person and its same beauty, but only the lover is transported—why? I cannot understand Menander's lines or conceive his meaning when he says: 'This malady is an occasion of the soul, and he that is smitten is wounded inwardly.' In fact the god is the cause: one he infects, and another he leaves free.

"And now 'forasmuch as it hath come to my lips' I feel I must not leave unspoken a theme whose proper place was the outset of my discourse, for it is a very important theme. It may be true of things in general of which we have cognition that they obtain their original credit with us, insofar as they are not perceived by the senses, in three ways: through myth, through law, and through reason. Of our belief in the gods it is certainly true that our guides and teachers are the poets, the lawgivers, and thirdly the philosophers. That the gods exist all of these agree; but in their number, order, essence, and powers they differ greatly with one another. The gods of the philosophers are 'Without disease or age, untouched by toil, not subject to the heavily moaning passage of Acheron.' Hence, unlike the poets, the philosophers do not admit the deity of Strife and Prayer, nor are they willing to acknowledge that Terror and Fear are gods and sons of Ares. In many respects the philosophers are at odds with the lawgivers also. Xenophanes, for example, bade the Egyptians not honor Osiris as a god if they believed him a mortal, and if they believed him a god not to bewail him. On the other hand certain ideas and numbers of the philosophers, their monads and spirits which they consider to be gods, the poets and lawgivers have no patience to hear and no capacity to understand. In a word, then, opinions on the subject vary greatly and are in conflict with one another. Similarly there were once three factions in Athens—those of the shore, the highlands, the plain—who were at odds with one another and quarreled. But eventually all united and cast their ballots for Solon and together elected him to be mediator, magistrate, and lawgiver because he seemed incontestably to merit the palm of excellence. Just so the three factions on the question of the gods, though their opinions diverge and they cast disparate ballots and do not readily accept their rivals' candidates, nevertheless on one candidate they are solidly unanimous. The representative poets and lawgivers and philosophers alike enroll Love among the gods and 'with united acclaim praise him,' as Alcaeus says the Mytileneans chose Pittacus to be their ruler.

"For us Love is proclaimed king and magistrate and dictator by Hesiod and Plato and Solon. He is crowned and brought down from Helicon to the Academy, and he advances in state with many teams of friendship and communion, not, as Euripides says, 'yoked with fetters not of bronze,' making chill and dour constraint a covering for his need. Rather is this union borne aloft as on wings towards the fairest thing in all the world and the most divine. But this thing others have described better than I can do."

When my father had spoken, Soclarus said: "This is the second time, you will notice, that you have been about to treat of the same subject and then willfully somehow dodged and eluded it. If I may speak freely, I think you are shortchanging us in depriving us of that sacred discourse. A while ago you touched gingerly on Plato and the Egyptians and passed them by, and now you are doing the same thing. As to what 'has been notably said' by Plato, or rather by the Muses through Plato, my good friend, you need not repeat it even if we should bid you to. But as to your allusion to the Egyptian myth and your intimation that it corresponds to the Platonic doctrine of Love, you can no longer keep the matter in the dark but must clarify it. We shall be grateful to hear even a little on a great theme."

The others joined in the request, and so my father spoke: "Like the Greeks the Egyptians recognize two Loves, one common and the other heavenly; but they also believe in a third Love, which is the Sun, and they show great veneration for Aphrodite, whom they identify with moon and earth. We too perceive a great similarity between the sun and Love. Neither is fire, as some think, but the beam of sweet and fecund warmth which derives from the sun supplies the body it strikes with sustenance and light and growth, and that which derives from Love does the same for souls. Just as the sun is warmer when it emerges from clouds and fog, so is Love sweeter and keener when the beloved has been reconciled after anger and jealousy. Moreover, as certain people believe that the sun kindles and is extinguished, so some suppose the same thing about Love, as being mortal and unstable. And finally, neither can a physical constitution which is not trained endure the sun without pain, nor a temper with soul uneducated. Body and soul are alike troubled and made ill by the exposure, and each blames the power of the god rather than his own weakness.

"Yet in this one respect would they seem to differ: the sun exhibits the fair and the ugly alike to the eyes of the beholder, whereas Love's light illumines only the fair, and to the fair only does he persuade lovers to turn and gaze; the rest they disregard.

"The earth, we should say, has no likeness to Aphrodite, but those who call the moon Aphrodite have hit upon a meaningful analogy. The moon is earthy and heavenly, a region where the immortal is mingled with the mortal, feeble in itself and dark when the sun does not irradiate it —as is Aphrodite when Love is not present.

"The moon's resemblance to Aphrodite and the sun's to Love is accordingly stronger than their resemblance to any other gods, but this resemblance is by no means an identity. Body is not identical with soul, and they are apprehended differently, as the sun and Love are, the former through perception, the latter through cognition. Without meaning to appear overacute one might say that the action of the sun is opposite to that of Love. The sun diverts the understanding from things apprehended through cognition to things perceived by the senses. It enchants us by the grace and splendor of its aspect and persuades us to seek for all things, including truth itself, in and around itself and nowhere else. 'So we find ourselves hopelessly in love, with the thing we see, this world of brightness,' as Euripides [*Hippolytus* 193-5] says, 'because we have no experience of any other mode of living' —or rather because we have forgotten the things of which Love effects recollection.

"Just as upon awakening into a bright and dazzling light all the images which appeared in our dreams depart and disperse, so when we change from another world to this the sun seems to paralyze our memory and enchant our intelligence, so that pleasure and admiration cause forgetfulness of our former existence. And yet the truth is that the wakeful state of the soul is in that other life, and when it arrives here it is in a dream state, in which it is astonished at the sun and greets it as the fairest and most divine of all dreams. 'About it pour forth dreams charming but deceitful,' and it is persuaded that everything here is lovely and precious, unless it encounters divine and chaste Love to be its physician and deliverer. Love arriving by way of the body to be its guide to truth leads it from Hades to the 'field of truth,' where beauty abundant and pure and unadulterated is established. Those who have long yearned to embrace this beauty and be joined to it Love leads on with kindly escort, like the mystagogue who assists at initiation.

"But of those who are sent below again Love cannot lead the soul directly but only through the body. Teachers of geometry fashion tangible and visible imitations of spheres, cubes, and dodecahedrons and hold them before their pupils who are not yet able to apprehend notions of incorporeal and unaffectable being. Similarly heavenly Love contrives for us fair images of what is fair. To be sure these images are mortal instead of divine, subject to affects instead of unaffectable, perceptible to the senses instead of purely cognitive, yet by these forms and colors and general appearances he displays the shining bloom of youth, and when recollection is first kindled by these means Love gradually stirs it into full memory.

"Many, because of the ineptitude of family and friends, endeavor to extinguish the passion forcibly and unreasonably. The result is that they enjoy no benefit but either fill themselves with smoke and confusion or rush into shady and illicit pleasures and wither ingloriously away. Others using prudence and reason have removed the raging flame, precisely as one does to a fire, with due regard, and have retained in their soul a glow and light and warmth. Nor does this warmth, as has been alleged, produce a convulsion of sperm and a rush of atoms pressed together by lightness and titillation. Rather does it produce a marvelous fecund suffusion, as in a burgeoning plant which is well nurtured. It opens pores of complaisance and affection, and in no long while we pass beyond the body of the beloved and are borne inward to lay hold of his character which our eyes, with blindfold now removed, can perceive. We enter into close association with him, in words and deeds, provided he possesses in his spirits some vestige of likeness of what is fair. If not we let him go and turn to others, just as bees leave behind many fresh flowers which have no honey. But if he does possess some trace of the divine, some emanation, some pulsing similitude, then on an eager transport of pleasure and admiration we recover memory and again kindle with that true supernal love which is blessed and beloved of all and dear.

"The poets who have written about the god seem for the most part to have dealt frivolously with him or to have composed their songs in revelry. Occasionally they have spoken seriously, whether as result of reason and reflection or because they hit upon the truth with divine help. That is the case of the verses relative to the god's birth: 'That most redoubtable of the gods Iris of the goodly sandals bore when she had lain with Zephyr of the golden locks.' But perhaps you have been convinced by the grammarians who explain the expression as an allusion to the variety and fresh vigor of the passion."

"Can there be any other explanation?" asked Daphnaeus.

"Then listen," said my father; "the evidence for what I say is compelling. The phenomenon of the rainbow [Iris] is due to refraction. When our vision encounters a cloud which is somewhat moist, smooth, and of moderate thickness, and we see the reflection of the sun upon it together with the shining rays of the sun which surround it, the effect upon us is that the spectacle is actually in the cloud. The clever mechanism of Love with reference to souls which are noble and devoted to beauty is similar. In the appearances of beauty which we celebrate here he produces a reflection whereby recollection leads to that supernal beauty which is divine and lovable and truly blessed and admirable.

"But most people pursue that imagined phantom of beauty reflected in boys and women, as in a mirror, and when they have seized it can secure nothing more solid than pleasure mixed with pain. But this is like the dazed and distracted Ixion, who was searching for the empty object of his desire in the clouds as if fumbling in shadows. So children eager to seize the rainbow in their hands grasp at a mere appearance.

"Very different is the character of a gifted and prudent lover. Him refraction bears upward to divine and cognitive beauty. Beauty of the corporeal body which he encounters serves him merely as an instrument of recollection. He welcomes and embraces this beauty, but the joy of associating with it is surpassed by the kindled ardor of his intellect. Neither when their bodies are united in this life do such lovers sit quietly admiring the light they crave, nor when they have gone yonder after death do they strive to escape and turn back to this world, to writhe at the chamber doors of the newly married, like nightmare phantoms of men and women abandoned to carnal pleasure and not fit to be styled lovers. But the true lover when he reaches yonder region and converses with beauty, as it is lawful for him to do, becomes winged and is continuously devoted to the ecstatic mysteries of his own god, joyously dancing and ministering to him, until such time as he proceeds to the meadows of the moon and Aphrodite to fall asleep and begin a new birth.

"But such matters," my father continued, "go beyond the subject of our present discourse. Like the other gods Love, as Euripides [*Hippolytus* 7] says, 'is pleased when respected by mankind' and offended when he is not. Most kindly is he to those who receive him fittingly, and grievous to those who show him contumely. Zeus of strangers is not so swift in chastising injuries done to guests and suppliants nor Zeus of kindred in heeding the curses of a father, as is Love in hearkening to injured lovers and punishing the ill-bred and disdainful.

"There is surely no need to repeat the story of Euxynthetus and Leucocome, or that of her still called the Peeper in Cyprus. But the story of the Cretan Gorgo perhaps you have not heard. Gorgo's fate was very like the Peeper's, except that she was turned into stone when she peeped out the window to see her lover being carried to his grave. A young man named Asander fell in love with this Gorgo. He was a likely young man and of good birth, but he had fallen from a flourishing state into poverty and lowliness. Nevertheless he did not undervalue himself but asked Gorgo, who was his kinswoman, to be his wife, though she had many suitors and there was great rivalry for her hand because of her wealth. And yet numerous and worthy as his rivals were, Asander persuaded all the girl's guardians and relatives. . . ."

[*Here there is a break in the text. In the portion missing the story of Gorgo was concluded, Zeuxippus inveighed against conjugal love, and the company started back for Thespiae from the shrine of the Muses. When the text resumes Plutarch is again the speaker and is rebutting the position of Zeuxippus.*]

". . . Moreover the causes to which they ascribe the genesis of Love are not peculiar to either sex but common to both. They allege that atoms organized in his likeness proceed from the beloved, enter the body of the lover, and by their scurrying about stir and titillate the mass, swelling into seed to peculiar configurations: can it be that configurations of atoms may derive from women but not from boys? If those fair and holy recollections which invite us to that supernal, divine, and true and Olympian beauty by which the soul acquires wings can be evoked by boys and striplings, what is to prevent their being evoked by girls and women when a pure and seemly character is manifested in the bloom and grace of form? Just as a well-made shoe reveals the comeliness of the foot, as Ariston says, those with keen perception of such merits can discern the splendid footprints of the soul, upright and untainted, laid up in handsome figures and pure bodies.

"The voluptuary [in the play] who was asked, 'To the feminine dost rather incline, or to the masculine?' answered, 'Wherever beauty is: I am ambidextrous.' That is a proper answer for a lustful man. But surely a noble lover of beauty should direct his love towards true beauty and comeliness and not according to the distinguishing marks of sex. A lover of horses admires the comeliness of 'Aithe, Agamemnon's mare' no less than the stallion Podargos, and a hunting man takes pleasure not only in dogs but cares for Cretan and Spartan bitches also. And shall the beauty-loving lover of mankind not be impartially and equally disposed to both sexes? Shall he imagine that there is a distinction between the love of men and women as there is in their clothing? It is said that 'beauty is the flower of virtue.' To say that this flower never blooms in women and that they never manifest a natural tendency towards virtue is absurd. Aeschylus was right when he said, 'A young woman who hath tasted of man I can recognize by the light in her eye.' Is it possible that the marks of a bold and incontinent and corrupt character are obvious to the eye in the case of women, while decency and chastity add no glow to their beauty? Or if these qualities are plainly manifest, is it possible that they should not awaken and invite love? Neither hypothesis is either true or reasonable.

"All these qualities, it has been shown, pertain to both sexes in common. And since a common defense must be undertaken for both, my dear Daphnaeus, let us combat the arguments which Zeuxippus has just now alleged. He has identified Love with unbridled desire which sweeps the soul towards wantonness. That is indeed not his own conviction, but he has repeatedly heard it from men morose and dour. Of these some have married wretched women with some pittance of dowry and then flung them and their money into household drudgery and sordid bookkeeping; consequently they chafe at the yoke daily and treat them as chattels. Others want children more than they do wives. Like cicadas who discharge their seed on an onion or other such vegetable, they quickly impregnate whatever bodies they chance upon and when they have harvested the crop they say goodbye to the marriage, or if they continue in it take no thought of it and set no value on loving and being loved.

"In my judgment the difference of a single letter between *stergesthai* or *stergein* ['to be loved,' 'to love'] and *stegein* ['to keep'] denotes at once the mutual kindliness begotten of time and the bond of habit. That union which is brought about by the stroke and inspiration of Love will, in the first place, know no distinction between Mine and Thine, as in the *Republic* of Plato. The saying 'friends share all things' does not apply in any simple sense even to lovers, but only to those who, separated in body, press their souls together and fuse them into one, and no longer wish to be, or believe that they are, two. Secondly, in regard to the mutual faithfulness essential to marriage, that which is imposed from without by prescription of the laws has more of constraint than voluntary fidelity. It is enforced by shame and fear, 'it needeth many a bridle, many a curb,' which must be applied to spouses. But Love possesses such great self-mastery and decency and good faith that even when he encounters an incontinent spirit he diverts him from other lovers, trims down his impudence, and crushes his insolent pride; instead Love implants modesty and silence and tranquility, and clothes the lover with a posture of comeliness and renders him attentive to a single love.

"You must surely have heard tell of the famous Lais,

whom many loved and who was celebrated in song. She
set all Greece afire with love of her, or rather she was
fought over by the two seas. But when she herself was
touched by love for Hippolochus the Thessalian, 'forsak-
ing Acrocorinth washed of green waves,' she secretly ran
away from her numerous crowd of lovers and forsook the
great army of courtesans to follow a decent path. But the
women of Thessaly were jealous of her beauty and envied
her; they brought her into a sanctuary of Aphrodite and
there stoned her to death. That is apparently the reason
the sanctuary is called Aphrodite the Slayer's to this day

"We know too of lowly serving-women who avoid con-
sorting with their masters and of private individuals who
scorn the embraces of queens when they have once got
Love as masters of their souls. Just as it is told of Rome
when a dictator is appointed all the other magistrates lay
down their office, so when Love becomes lord over anyone he is freed from other masters and rulers and released
to the sole service of the god, like a slave made over to
a temple. A true woman lawfully united to a husband
through Love would sooner abide the embraces of bears
and serpents than the touch and carnal intimacy of a
strange man.

"Though there is a great abundance of instances, especially among you who are fellow-countrymen of the god
and members of his fraternity, nevertheless to omit the
tale of Camma the Galatian would not be right. Camma
was a woman of transcendent beauty and was married to
the tetrarch Sinatus. Sinorix, the most powerful of the
Galatians, conceived a passion for her and killed Sinatus,
for as long as Sinatus was alive he could neither persuade
the woman nor force her. Camma found a refuge and a
solace for her affliction in serving as priestess of Artemis,
an office hereditary in her family. Most of her time she
devoted to the service of the goddess, and admitted no
one to her presence, though many princes and grandees
sought her in marriage. And when Sinorix made bold to
approach her on the subject of marriage she did not evade
his suit nor did she upbraid him for what he had done,

as if Sinorix had been driven to his deed, not by any wickedness, but solely by affection and desire for her. He therefore addressed her with confidence and asked to marry her. She responded to his advances, took him by the hand, led him to the altar of the goddess, and poured a libation cup of hydromel from a flask which, as later appeared, had been drugged with poison. Then when she had herself drunk half the cup she handed the rest to the Galatian. And when she saw that he had drained it she uttered a loud cry of joy and called upon her deceased husband by name. 'It was in expectation of this day, my dearest husband,' said she, 'that I have endured my wretched life apart from you. Now receive me with joy. For your sake I have taken vengeance on this vilest of men. Gladly did I share life with you, gladly do I share death with him.' Sinorix was carried out on a litter and died shortly after, but Camma survived a day and a night and is then said to have died with great resolution and cheerfulness.

"Considering the great number of analogous cases, both among ourselves and among the barbarians, how shall we tolerate those who revile Aphrodite and allege that her union with and assistance to Love prevents the development of friendship? It is rather the association, or more properly, the lasciviousness and excesses, of male with male of which the sound-minded observer should say, 'Lo, froward Hybris is here at work, not Cypris.'

"Those who are pleased to serve as catamites, therefore, we reckon in the vilest class of baseness and upon them we bestow no jot of faith or respect or friendship; as Sophocles truly says: 'Those devoid of such friends as these rejoice; they that have them pray to lose them.' Some, on the other hand, are not naturally vile, but have been deceived or compelled to prostitute themselves and serve as catamites; there is no class of men for whom they have more persistent suspicion and hatred than their pederasts, and when opportunity offers they exact a terrible vengeance. Archelaus was killed by Crateas, who had been made his minion, and Alexander of Pherae by Pytholaus. Periander, tyrant of Ambracia, asked his minion whether he were not yet with child, and the lad was so infuriated that he killed him.

"But for married women physical intimacies are the seeds of friendship; they are the sharing of great and sacred mysteries. The aspect of physical pleasure is brief, but from it there burgeons day by day consideration and complaisance and mutual affection and trust. The Delphians cannot be charged with silliness for giving Aphrodite the epithet 'harmony-bringing,' nor can Homer for calling conjugal intercourse 'friendship.' Evidence of Solon's expertness in legislating for matrimony is provided by his prescription that a man must lie with his wife at least three times a month. The object was not pleasure; but just as states renew their covenants with one another from time to time, Solon desired that the marriage bond be renewed by such tenderness after the accumulation of daily complaints.

"But, it will be objected, love of women gives rise to base and crazy conduct. Ah, but does not love of boys give rise to even worse? 'When I look upon him I lose my native character.' 'Ah, beardless, luscious, pretty youth!' 'Clinging to him would I die, and win my epitaph.' Actually, neither the mad passion for women nor mad passion for boys can be called love.

"To declare that women have no share in excellence is therefore an absurdity. What need to speak of their prudence and understanding or even of their faith and justice, when so many of them have manifested courage and fortitude and greatness of spirit? And when we can find no fault with the quality of their character in other respects it is very strange indeed to insist that it is incapable only of friendship. Women love their children and love their husbands; they are rich in affection, like a fertile soil receptive to the seed of friendship, and endowed with charm and grace. Just as poesy by fitting honeyed melody and measure and rhythm to discourse renders it more efficacious for communicating instruction and more irresistible when it is harmful, so nature by clothing woman with a gracious glance and a persuasive voice and a winning form and figure, has given to the wanton effective means for voluptuousness and seduction, but to the chaste great resources for benevolence and friendship to her husband.

"This was the point of Plato's advice to Xenocrates. Xenocrates was a sound and stalwart man but rather morose in character, so Plato urged him to sacrifice to the Graces. A good and chaste woman might similarly be advised to sacrifice to Love, so that he might favor her marriage with his propitious presence and adorn her with all feminine attractions, to the end that her husband might not roam off to another woman and then be compelled to say, like the man in the comedy, 'What a wretch I am to injure such a wife!' In marriage to love is a greater good than to be loved, for love forestalls many faults, indeed all the faults which mar and ruin marriage.

"The mordant sensation which attends initial intercourse, my dear Zeuxippus, you must not fear like a wound or gash. And yet even a wound is no terrible price for growing into oneness with a good woman, like the grafting of a tree. A wound is also the inception of a pregnancy. There can be no complete fusion of two persons unless each has been affected by the force of the other.

"Elementary lessons perplex children beginning their education, and philosophy confuses young men; but neither in those cases does the sting persist nor in the case of lovers. Love is like a combination of two liquids: at first the mixture seems confused and produces an effervescence, but in course of time it settles and is clarified and takes on an enduring stability. The union of lovers is the sort of mixture which is correctly called a complete amalgam. But the associations of persons who merely live together are like the contacts and concatenations of Epicurus' atoms; they undergo strong attractions and repulsions but never produce such a oneness as does Love when he lays hold of a wedded union. Pleasures derived from others are not so great nor are advantages conferred upon others so consistent, nor is the beauty of any other friendship so glorious and enviable 'as when man and wife with single mind and heart keep house together' [*Odyssey* 6.183].

"The law fosters such unions, and nature points out that

even the gods have need of love for the sake of shared procreation of the race. And so the poets say that 'Earth felt
loving desire of showers,' and heaven of earth; and the
physicists declare that the sun is in love with the moon and
consorts with it and impregnates it. And forasmuch as
Earth is the mother of all mankind and all animal creation
and all vegetation, would not all birth and begetting perforce one day cease and be wholly extinguished if powerful
love or yearning of the god should forsake matter and matter thereupon cease to desire and pursue the impulses and
motions which derive from Love?

"But we must not give the impression of wandering too
far afield or indulging in footless fancies. You know very
well that the inconstancy of pederastic attachments is a
common subject for reproach and raillery. People say that
such friendships are severed by a hair, like an egg, and
that they are like nomad shepherds who spend the spring
in verdant and flowery meadows and then break up camp,
as from an enemy country. Bion the sophist used a coarser
phrase, calling the whiskers of minions Harmodiuses and
Aristogitons [the tyrannicides], for by that hair their lovers
were liberated from a pretty tyranny. But such a reproach
cannot be laid to true lovers. Euripides expressed it neatly
when he embraced and kissed the handsome Agathon,
whose beard was already sprouted; 'beauty,' said he, 'continues beautiful even in its autumn.' But the love of virtuous women not only undergoes no autumn, but flourishes
even with hoary head and wrinkles and abides forever in
tombs and monuments. Very few unions of male lovers
have endured, but of men and women joined in love we
can count myriads of cases where unions wholly faithful
have been maintained loyally and eagerly to the end. I
should like to cite at least one example which occurred
in my time, in the reign of the Emperor Vespasian.

"Civilis, the prime mover of the insurrection in Gaul,
naturally had many confederates, among whom was Sa-
binus, a young man of good birth whose wealth and reputation made him the most distinguished of the Gauls. The
great conspiracy which they attempted failed, and so real-
izing the punishment that awaited them some took their

On Brotherly Love

Plutarch's own strong family feeling is evident throughout his works. He appears to have had a genius for friendship, and it is significant that (in the third paragraph of the present treatise) he defines friendship as nature's surrogate for the love of family. As in his other essays Plutarch makes large use of earlier writers, but *Brotherly Love* has an unusually personal note. He makes a point of mentioning his own brother Timon, evidently with the notion of emulating Plato who immortalized his brothers Glaucon and Adimantus by mentioning them in the best of his dialogues. Its warmth and its numerous ancedotes make this a particularly attractive essay.

THEIR ANCIENT FIGURES of the Dioscuri the Spartans called Docana or Beams: these are two timbers standing parallel with one another and joined by two transverse timbers. The configuration of this dedication, shared and indivisible, seems an appropriate symbol for the fraternal love of these deities. Just so, my dear Nigrinus and Quintus, do I dedicate this treatise on brotherly love to you who are worthy of it as a shared offering. The subject of its instruction you yourselves already practice, so that you will seem rather to be invoked as witnesses than admonished. The pleasure you take in your correct practice will make you persevere in it the more firmly when it is buttressed by rational judgment and you perceive that it is approved by sound and scrupulous observers. Aristarchus, father of Theodectes, in jesting at the hordes of sophists, remarked that in the old days barely seven sages were known whereas nowadays it is not easy to find as many laymen. For myself I observe that brotherly love is as great a rarity as brotherly hatred was in the old days; so paradoxical did the phenomenon appear that life relegated it to the tragic stage. But nowadays if men encounter good brothers they are no less astonished than at the spectacle of the Molion twins, whose bodies appeared to have grown together. To enjoy property and friends and servants in common seems to them as monstrous as for one soul to avail itself of the hands and feet and eyes of two bodies.

And yet Nature herself has supplied a paradigm for brotherly partnership, and an easy one. In the body itself it has contrived that most of the necessary members are paired, like brothers, or rather twins—hands, feet, eyes, ears, nostrils—thus making it plain that all such divisions are for the sake of mutual safety and cooperation, not of dissidence and contention. The hands nature has cleft into numerous and unequal fingers, thus making of them the most exact and craftsmanlike tools. This is what induced old Anaxagoras to attribute the source of human wisdom and understanding to the hands; but the truth of the matter is just the opposite. It is not because man has hands that he is wise; but because he is by nature rational and ingenious, by nature he obtained these tools. So much is obvious to all: from one seed and a single source nature produces two, three, or more brothers, not for discord and rivalry but in order that being disparate they might better assist one another. Those three-bodied and hundred-handed creatures, if ever indeed they existed, were grown together in all their parts and hence incapable of separate activity outside the single body. But for brothers it is possible to abide at home or travel abroad together, or to engage in public life or in agriculture with each assisting the other—that is, if they preserve the good will and harmony with which nature originally endowed them. If they do not they are no different, in my judgment, from feet which trip one another up or fingers which unnaturally tangle and twist one another. Or better, just as in a single body in which breath and sustenance are shared, common intent and purpose mingle moist and dry and cold and hot into a wholesome and agreeable constitution and temperament, "without which," as the saying is, "neither wealth nor kingly sway which exalts men to gods" gives pleasure or profit. If rivalry and strife should arise among its members, the living creature is foully corrupted and destroyed;

just so because of the concord of brethren family and household are sound and flourishing, friends and familiars like a well-trained chorus do and say and think nothing inept. "But amidst dissension even the scoundrel obtains honor"—a slandering slave, an alien flatterer who worms his way in, an evil-eyed citizen. Just as diseases induce cravings for strange and injurious viands in bodies which have lost desire for their proper food, so ill will and suspicion of relatives induce vile and wicked associations to fill the empty place from without.

The Arcadian seer of whom Herodotus tells contrived himself a wooden leg of necessity, because he had lost his own. But when brother quarrels with brother and gets himself some stranger from the market square or exercise field for a friend he would seem actually to be doing no less than voluntarily hewing away a portion of his natural flesh and attaching some alien substitute in its place. Our very need to seek out and acquire friendship and companionship teaches us to honor and cultivate and preserve ties of kinship, for we are neither able nor by nature fitted to live solitary, without friends and without companionship. And so Menander correctly says: "Not from our cups and daily indulgences, father, do we find a man to whom we may entrust our life's concerns; a much greater windfall doth a man deem it if he but find the shadow of a friend." Shadows indeed are the majority of friendships, mere imitations and phantoms of that primal bond which nature has implanted in sons towards their fathers and in brothers towards their brothers. And if a man do not revere and acknowledge that bond, what pledge of good will can he give to strangers? Or what sort of man is he who in greetings and letters addresses his comrade as "brother" but thinks it improper to walk the same road with his true brother? To adorn a brother's picture while beating and mutilating his person is madness; similarly to revere and acknowledge the title of brother in others while hating and avoiding an actual brother is neither the mark of a sane man nor of one to whom it has ever occurred that nature is a very holy thing and the greatest of sanctuaries.

When I was in Rome I recall that I undertook to arbitrate between two brothers. One of them was reputed to be a philosopher; but his title of philosopher, as it turned out, was no less spurious and counterfeit than his title of brother. When I asked him to behave like a philosopher to a brother and a layman, he said, "Such a remark truly befits a layman. For my part I attach no particular value to the fact that we were born of the same womb."

"You make it clear enough," I replied, "that you attach no particular value to being born of the same womb." But all other men, even if they think otherwise, repeat in speech and in verse that next after the gods nature and the law which follows nature has bestowed first and greatest honor upon parents. There is nothing men can do more pleasing to the gods than gladly and eagerly pay out to their parents and nurses their debts of long standing as well as their newer obligations. Nor, on the other hand, can there be any clearer proof of godlessness than neglect and cruelty to parents. Hence to mistreat others is indeed forbidden; but not to bring one's mother and father happiness by deeds and words, even if one refrains from causing them pain, is regarded as impious and lawless. And what act or attention or disposition on the part of their children is better calculated to bring parents happiness than consistent good will and love for a brother?

This principle is easy to apprehend from lesser cases. When the sons of a house abuse a homeborn slave whom the father or mother esteems, or when they neglect plants and fields in which they took pleasure, they cause their parents distress. A homeborn dog or horse that is uncared for touches the affection and pride of older people, and they are grieved when their children despise and hiss at entertainments and spectacles and sporting events which they themselves have admired. Can they then bear it with equanimity when their sons are at odds and hate and curse one another and are always opposed to one another in every enterprise and every transaction and are ruined by one another? One would hardly think so. But on the other hand when brothers are affectionate and loving towards one another, and their emotions and actions reflect the close union which nature has imposed upon them, when they share their discussions and pastimes and amusements with one another, then their brotherly love provides a sweet and blessed nurture for their parents' old age. No father has ever been so fond of discourse or of honor or of money as he is fond of his children; and therefore fathers take no such pleasure in seeing their sons eloquent or rich or powerful as in seeing them loving one another. Apollonis of Cyzicus, mother of King Eumenes and three other sons, to wit, Attalus, Philetaerus, and Athenaeus, is said to have felicitated herself and thanked the gods, not for wealth or royal sway, but because she saw her three younger sons guarding the eldest while he moved among them without fear though they were armed with spears and swords. On the other hand, when Xerxes discovered that his son Ochus was plotting against his brothers he died of grief. "Hard are the wars of brothers," as Euripides has said, and hardest of all for their parents. When a man is at odds with his own brother and hates him, it must necessarily follow that he finds fault with him that begot that brother and her that gave him birth.

Pisistratus took a second wife when his sons were grown, saying that inasmuch as he thought his sons fine and upstanding he wished to become the father of more such. Good and just sons not only have greater love for one another because of their parents, but also love their parents for each other's sake. They always believe and declare that they owe a debt of gratitude to their parents for many things, but most of all for their brothers. This is the sweetest and dearest of all the gifts they acquire from their parents. Very fitly does Homer represent Telemachus as reckoning his want of a brother a calamity [*Odyssey* 16.117]: "My race has Cronus' son made solitary." Hesiod is wrong in advising that one sole son should inherit his father's goods, and yet Hesiod was disciple of the Muses, who got their name because mutual good will and sisterly love bound them together [*homou ousai*].

With respect to parents then, brotherly love has this quality: love of a brother is direct proof of love of father and mother. And with respect to a brother's children it is an incomparable lesson and pattern for brotherly love. On the other hand, children are very ready to follow the bad pattern furnished by brotherly animosity. A man grown gray in litigation and strife and contention with his brothers who then admonishes his sons to live in concord with one another is like "Himself festering with sores would be physician to others." His deeds stultify his words. The Theban Eteocles rants to his brother [Euripides, *Phoenician Women* 504 ff.]: "To the rising of the sun would I mount, to the very stars, and then descend below earth were I but able to achieve this, could I possess kingship, the gods' greatest boon." If, after such an utterance, he admonished his own sons in this fashion [*ibid.* 536]: "Give honor to equality; it binds friends to friends, cities to cities, allies to allies. This bond alone is wont to abide among mankind"—who is there who would not despise him? Or what sort of man was Agamemnon if after feasting his brother with the flesh of his brother's children he had given his own sons this sententious advice: "Only the uses of friendship based on blood are wont to abide when evil overflows."

Hatred of brothers is therefore a bad nurse of old age and a worse nurse of children; it must be purged away. It is also a source of obloquy and suspicion to a man's fellow-citizens. They cannot suppose that such enmity and hostility could arise after brothers have been brought up together in intimate familiarity unless each was privy to many wicked deeds committed by the other. The dissolution of great good will and love must imply some great cause, and hence it comes about that reconciliation is never easy. Objects that are merely welded together are capable of being reunited and rejoined even if the solder is loosened, but when the natural unity of a body is split and broken, it is very hard to solder and reunite the parts. So friendships formed for expediency's sake can be easily reunited if they come disjoined, but brothers who fall out of the attachment which is natural to them cannot easily be brought together again. Even if they are brought together the rift continues to fester in its loathsome if hidden scar. Now any enmity between man and man involves the most spirited of passions—ambition, anger, envy, sense of injury—and vexes a man with pain and excitement. But when enmity is directed against a brother, who must needs participate in the same sacrifices and ancestral rites, who must share burial ground and live in the same or a neighboring house, the grief cries out for attention. Daily it emphasizes the mad folly which transforms the most intimate of figures and dearest of faces into the most unwelcome and makes a detestable sound of a voice which was sweet and familiar from boyhood. They see other pairs of brothers enjoying the same house and table, their lands and slaves undivided, and they themselves keep different friends and associates and regard as distasteful anything their brother welcomes. Anyone may very easily calculate that new friends and boon companions, new connections and familiars, may be acquired, when the old, like worn-out tools and implements, are gone. But for a brother there can be no substitute, just as there cannot be for a hand that has been amputated or an eye that has been struck out. Truly did that Persian lady declare [Herodotus 3.119], when she preferred to save her brother's life instead of her children, that she could acquire other children, but that, her parents being deceased, she could have no other brother.

What should one say, it may be asked, if one happens to have a bad brother? In the first place it must be borne in mind that badness inheres in every kind of relationship. "Scrutinize the greatest part of mortality," says Sophocles, "and you will find baseness." Close examination will discover that no bond of family, of friendship, or of love is uncomplicated, untroubled, and pure of any taint. The Spartan who married a tiny wife explained that one must choose the least of the evil. But brothers should be prudently advised to endure the most familiar of evils rather than make trial of strange ones. The former course is irreproachable because it is obligatory; the latter, being voluntary, is blameworthy. A crony or classmate or guest is not "bound by brassless fetters of shame," but one who has shared your blood and nurture, who has the same father and the same mother, is so bound. For his sake it is proper to overlook certain failings. To his brother a man should say [*Odyssey* 13.331], "I cannot forsake you in your wretchedness," when he sins or is bad and foolish, lest hatred inadvertently inflict punishment too hard and severe upon a failing inherited from the seed of a common father and mother. In passing sentence upon strangers, as Theophrastus says, love must not take precedence over judgment but judgment over love. But where nature need not impose affection as a control of judgment, and need not wait for the proverbial bushel of salt to be shared, but has already begotten the sprout of love, there we must not be too severe, we must not be too rigorous in censuring faults. What is one to say of people who readily tolerate and are amused at faults of strangers and visitors whose acquaintance has been scraped up at some bar or game or sporting event, and then show themselves angry and implacable to their brothers? Or of people who feed and fondle ill-tempered dogs and horses, even lynxes, cats, monkeys, and lions, and then refuse to tolerate anger or ignorance or pride in their own brothers? Or of others who give title to houses and fields to their mistresses and whores, and then stubbornly quarrel with their brothers over some corner of floor space? And then they give hatred of brothers the fine name of hatred of wickedness, and they go about charging their brothers with wickedness and complaining of them, while they are never offended with the same faults in others but associate with them on terms of intimacy.

Let this then serve as the preamble to my whole discourse. I shall make my instruction begin not as others do with the distribution of the father's estate, but with the rivalry and envy of which sons are guilty when their parents are yet alive. The Spartan ephors laid a fine upon Agesilaus for always sending an ox as a prize to any elder who had distinguished himself; they alleged as their reason that this was demagoguery and currying favor with the multitude. A son should be advised to show his parents attention but not by way of winning them over and turning their good will to himself. Many men have used such demagoguery to supplant their brothers and have put a fair but dishonest title to this greed. They deprive their brother of the greatest and fairest good in their father's gift, good will. Like sly and unprincipled rogues they creep upon their brothers and seize an opportune moment when they are occupied to attack their folly; they show themselves particularly observant and obedient and prudent in matters in which they observe shortcomings, real or apparent, in their brothers. But the contrary course should be followed. When the father is angry a brother should shoulder and share his brother's burden and by contributing his effort render it lighter; in the services and attentions he shows his father he should by all means make his brother a partner, and if his brother has neglected some occasion or attention he should exculpate him on the grounds that his character is more usefully engaged in loftier matters. Agamemnon puts the matter admirably [*Iliad* 10.122]: " 'Tis not for sloth nor a foolish heart that he stays; 'tis to me he looks, awaiting mine onset," adding that his brother had given him proper advice. Fathers gladly accept euphemisms and willingly trust their sons; they will call a brother's sluggishness ingenuousness, his awkwardness uprightness, his touchiness pride. Hence the reconciler has two advantages: he mollifies his father's annoyance with his brother, and he increases his father's good will towards himself.

And now when a man has thus exculpated his brother he should address himself to him and reprimand him sharply for his offense and frankly point out where he has fallen short. It is not right to give a brother's failings free license, but neither is it right to overwhelm the offender: the latter course befits a man who rejoices at his fellow's discomfiture, the former is tantamount to complicity in the offense. He that admonishes must show concern and share the culprit's distress. One who has proven an ardent advocate of his brother's cause before his parents is entitled to chide the brother himself with severity. But if a father find fault with one brother who is innocent of all offense, it is right for the other brother to be complaisant to the father in other respects and to bear all his displeasure and anger; but to remonstrate with parents on behalf of a brother and justify him when he is unfairly maligned and mistreated is a fine thing and free of all reproach. There is no need to fear being chided with the line of Sophocles [*Antigone* 742], "Cursed son, will you dispute with your father?" when a man frankly speaks his mind on behalf of a brother he believes unfairly treated. In such a litigation being proven wrong affords parents greater pleasure than a victory would.

When the father is dead it is right for brothers to unite in mutual affection more closely than before. Their partnership of love should be manifested at once in their shared tears and shared grief. They should repel the suspicions of servants and the calumnies of men who would ingratiate themselves with one or the other. They should put credit in the tales of brotherly love which are told of the Dioscuri, and in the story that a blow from Polydeuces' fist killed a fellow who tried to whisper slanders against his brother in his ear. And when they come to the division of their patrimony let them not declare war against one another, as the many do—"Hark the cry, War's daughter!"—ready armed for hostile encounter. On that day in particular they must use caution, for to some it is the source of implacable dissension and enmity, and to others of love and concord. Better it is that they alone, or if need be with some common friend assessor for both, acknowledging the lots of justice of which Plato speaks, should give and take on the basis of what is amicable and appropriate, considering that what is being divided is the guardianship and management while the use and possession of the property remains common to both and without division.

But those who overreach in the negotiations and wrest from each other nurses and slaves who have been brought up with them and have become their familiars do indeed depart richer by the price of a slave, but they have forfeited the dearest and most precious part of their heritage, a brother's trust and affection. Of some people we know that with no motive of greed but only for rivalry's sake they treat a patrimony as savagely as if they were plundering an enemy. Of this number were the Opuntians Chari-

cles and Antiochus; these men split a silver cup and ripped
a cloak and then went off as if some tragic curse had set
them on "to divide their household with a whetted sword"
[Euripides, *Phoenician Women* 68]. Some even recount
boastfully to third parties how they overreached their
brothers in a division by knavery, sharp dealing, and meretricious arguments; they had more fitly taken pleasure and
pride for having surpassed them in generosity and kindliness and giving ground.

Here it is proper to call Athenodorus to mind; all our
people remember him well. He had an elder brother named
Xenon, who was guardian over a large part of his property and wasted it. Finally he was condemned for committing rape upon a woman, and all his property was
confiscated to Caesar's treasury. Athenodorus was a stripling at the time; his beard had not yet sprouted. When a
portion of the property was made over to him he did not
disregard his brother, but placed all he had between
them and again shared with him. And though he was
much abused in the division he did not grow angry or
repent of what he had done, but bore his brother's folly,
which had become notorious throughout Greece, with
meekness and complacency.

In his utterances concerning the state Solon declared
that equality breeds no revolution. In substituting the
democratic and arithmetic reckoning for the superior geo-
metric he seemed too indulgent to the populace. But one
who offers counsel to brothers in a family ought particularly to erase Mine and Thine, as Plato advises his citizens
to do. If he cannot, he should counsel love of equality and
tenacity in maintaining it; thus he will lay a sound and
enduring foundation for peace and concord. To this end
he may make use of famous examples. Such, for instance,
is the reply of Pittacus to the Lydian king who inquired
whether he had money. "Twice as much as I should like,"
he said, "for my brother is dead." It is not merely that
the possession or lack of money causes enmity between
him that has more and him that has less; it is simply, as Plato says, that any inequality generates disturbance, whereas equality assures calmness and permanence.

Accordingly, any unevenness threatens dissension among brothers.

For brothers to be equal and undifferentiated in all things is, of course, impossible. In some respects their natures endow them unequally from the beginning, and in others their subsequent fortune; and such differences may produce envy and backbiting—ugly and fateful plagues which bring ruin not only upon families but upon whole cities. These must be guarded against, and if they nevertheless appear, remedied. The brother that excels must be advised, first of all, to share his accomplishments freely with his brothers; he should allow them to be clothed in his glory and participate in his friendships. If he is a powerful orator he should allow his brother use of this faculty as if it were no less his. Then he must never show pride or haughtiness, but by modesty and a retiring manner disburden his superiority of all envy and compensate for the inequality of fortune, so far as in him lies, by the moderation of his own bearing. Lucullus, for example, did not deem it right to hold a magistracy before his brother, though he was the elder, but let his own chance pass and waited for his brother's turn. Polydeuces preferred being a demigod with his brother to being a full god by himself, and retained a portion of mortality so that his brother might have a portion of immortality. In comparison you might he called very lucky, for without diminishing your own perquisites you are able to raise your brother to the same level and deck him with the same adornments, so that he can share your merits, your reputation, your good fortune. In this way Plato introduced his brothers into the finest of his writings, Glaucon and Adimantus in the *Republic,* and Antiphon, the youngest, in the *Parmenides*.

Moreover, if brothers are subject to inequality in their natures and fortunes, it follows that it is impossible for the one to excel the other altogether and in every respect. The elements, they say, derive from a common substance, and yet they exhibit the most diverse properties. But in the case of brothers sprung from one mother and the same father, no one has observed an instance where one combined all the Stoic virtues, being at once wise, handsome, graceful, liberal, esteemed, rich, eloquent, erudite, humane, while the other is awkward, ugly, despised, illiberal, needy, an impotent speaker, ignorant, and a misanthrope. Somehow even in the humblest and lowliest of things there is some portion of grace or power or innate capacity for some excellence. "Amid briers and thorny brambles there burgeon blooms of soft white lilies." Hence if a man who has won esteem in certain respects do not hinder or suppress whatever qualities his brother may have, and do not keep him from the first rank, as at some athletic contest, if he yield him ground and acknowledge that in many respects his brother is the better and more useful man, then he will extinguish all envy by removing its cause, like fuel from a fire, or rather he will never permit it to catch hold or make headway.

But even in fields where he has superiority a brother should seek his brother's assistance and counsel: if he is a rhetor, for example, in lawsuits; if he is a politician, in administering his office; if he holds some preferment, in bestowing honors. In a word, he should never permit him to be left out in any affair that is important or that carries dignity, but always make him a partner in whatever is honorable; he should use his assistance when he is present, and await his coming if he is not. He should make it plain that his brother is no less effective than himself, but only that his reputation and abilities are of a more retiring kind. By so doing he will diminish his own credit not one whit, but will add greatly to his brother's.

Advice of this sort should be given to the more eminent brother, but the inferior must be admonished also. He should be reminded that his brother is by no means the only person who is richer, more eloquent, or more brilliant in reputation than himself, and that myriads upon myriads of "mortals who feed on the fruits of the wide-wayed earth" have outstripped him. But if he persists in envying all of these, or if among so many that have succeeded only he that is nearest and dearest stings him, then he is surely the most wretched creature in the world.

Metellus gave it as his opinion that the Romans ought

to thank heaven that so admirable a man as Scipio had not been born in some other city. So everyone should of course aspire to distinguish himself by his merits, but failing to attain eminence, he ought to pray that his brother should achieve high superiority. But many people are so inept in their attitude towards excellence that they rejoice when their friends win distinction and are proud to number rich and powerful personages among their acquaintances, and yet consider that their brother's brilliance dims their own glory. They exult in the distinctions of their fathers and in the offices held by their grandfathers, in which they have no share or profit; but they are disheartened and humiliated by their brother's legacies and magistracies and brilliant marriages. To be sure, we ought to envy no one; but if this cannot be, we should turn our grudge elsewhere, towards strangers, like men who divert civil dissensions against a foreign enemy. As Diomedes said to Glaucus [*Iliad* 6.227], "There are many famous Trojans and their allies" against whom he could fight, and a Glaucus can find many other Achaeans to begrudge and vie with.

Brothers should not be like a scale where one pan is depressed when the other is raised, but like larger and smaller numbers in multiplication, where each multiplies and is multiplied; brothers should at once augment and be augmented by any advantage. The finger which is naturally unsuited to write or pluck the harp string is in no worse state than the fingers which do these things; all move together and somehow assist each other. It is as if they were purposely fashioned of unequal size and so arranged that the lesser should balance the larger and stronger. Thus Craterus, brother of King Antigonus, and Perilaus, brother of Cassander, devoted themselves to military and economic administration; but the Antiochuses and Seleucuses and again the Grypuses and the Cyzicenuses, who would not be schooled to take second place to their brothers but craved the purple and the diadem, brought great mischief upon one another and filled Asia with sorrow.

But since ambitious men are naturally envious and critical of those who surpass them in reputation and distinction, it is a most useful practice for brothers not to seek eminence and authority in the same field, but for each to pursue a different distinction. In the animal world those beasts who compete for the same food are at war with one another, and among athletes those who vie for the same prize are opponents, whereas boxers are friends with pancratiasts and long-distance runners are well-disposed to wrestlers. These are partisans of one another and eager for their friends' success. So of the Tyndarids Polydeuces won in boxing and Castor in the foot race. Homer represented Teucer as outstanding in archery, while his brother Ajax was eminent in the heavy infantry; the latter, he tells us admirably [*Iliad* 8.272], "sheltered his brother 'neath his shining shield." So in public service, generals rarely envy popular leaders, nor in rhetoric do lawyers envy display orators, nor in medicine do dietitians envy surgeons; rather do they take each other's part and commend each other.

But the effort to become famous and outstanding in the same craft or talent is no different among bad men than for two men to be in love with the same girl; each tries to get the upper hand, each tries to outdo the other. When walkers take different roads they can be of no help to one another; but when men follow different careers they not only banish envy but are of greater assistance to one another. Good instances are offered by Demosthenes and Chares, or Aeschines and Eubulus, and Hyperides and Leosthenes; one brother discoursed in public and wrote, and the other was active in civil or military administration. Hence brothers who are by nature unable to share reputation and talent without envy should make their pursuits and ambitions as divergent as possible, so that they may be able to afford each other pleasure, and not pain, by their success.

Besides all this one must be careful of the wicked talk of connections and relatives, sometimes even of one's own wife, to the effect that "Your brother runs everything, and everyone admires and waits on him; no one comes near you, no one pays you heed." But a prudent man would answer, "Yes, I have a famous brother, and I have a right to the greater part of his abilities." Socrates used to say that he would rather have Darius for a friend than a daric. In the view of a sensible brother, a brother who is a magistrate or who has attained distinction by wealth or eloquence is as desirable to have as wealth and office and eloquence. Such, then, are the ways in which inequalities between brothers may be mitigated.

But their ages too can be a source of dissension to brothers who are not well instructed. The elder naturally claim the right to rule over the younger and take precedence over them, and to have a larger share of reputation and authority, and so make themselves unpleasant and disagreeable. The younger, on the other hand, growing restive and spurning the curb, form the habit of disregarding and despising the elder. As a result the younger, feeling that they are begrudged and thwarted, avoid admonition and take it amiss, whereas the elder in their eagerness for superiority dread the advancement of the younger as implying their own decline.

In the cases of benefits conferred it is the common opinion that those who receive them should be more sensible of them and those who grant them less so; so with reference to age the elder should be admonished not to regard it too highly, and the younger not too lightly. In this way both would be delivered from superciliousness and neglect, from despising and being despised. The proper role for the elder is to be guardian and guide and counselor, and for the younger to respect, imitate, and heed; but let the elder's tutelage savor more of the comrade than of the father. Let him rather persuade than command, let him be readier to felicitate and applaud good conduct than to find fault if the younger miscarry and then chastise him; this is the more humane course. And as for the younger's heeding the elder's course, it should be by way of emulation, not competition, for emulation indicates admiration, whereas competition is a mark of envy. It follows that those who wish to be *like* themselves, people love, whereas they dislike and repress those who wish to be *equal* to themselves.

Among the many marks of respect which it is proper

for the young to show to their elders the most praise-
worthy is obedience; along with mutual respect obedience
gives rise to firm loyalty and reciprocal deference. Cato
showed his elder brother Caepio such obedience, gentle
and uncomplaining, from his earliest boyhood, and when
they were grown men Caepio showed Cato such deference
and such high regard that he said and did nothing without
Cato's knowledge. The story has been handed down that
Caepio had affixed his seal to the transcript of certain
testimony, and that Cato, arriving after this was done,
refused to add his own seal. Thereupon Caepio asked that
the document be returned, and removed his own seal from
it without inquiring what made his brother suspect the
testimony and distrust it.

The great respect which his brothers had for Epicurus
because of his kindliness and his care for them is shown
by their general attitude towards him and especially by
their enthusiastic devotion to his philosophy. From their
earliest youth they voiced their conviction that there had
never been anyone wiser than Epicurus. Even if their
judgment was wrong we must still admire both the man
who inspired such a conviction and the brothers who
maintained it. Indeed, even among more recent philosophers Apollonius the Peripatetic refuted the man who as-
serted that glory could not be shared by procuring an even
greater measure of glory for his younger brother Sotion.
In my own case I have many things for which I must be
grateful to fortune, but for the loyalty of my brother Timon
I am as grateful as for all the rest; no one that has had any
contact whatever with us can be ignorant of this, and
least of all you who are our close friends.

Brothers who are nearly of the same age are subject
to other disturbances which must be looked out for. These
are little things, to be sure, but numerous and frequent,
and they produce an evil impulse to irritate and provoke
which eventually develops into implacable rancor and
malice. They begin with disagreements in games, for example the feeding of pets, such as partridges and cocks,
and their fighting, then in the boys' competitions in the
gymnasium, backing dogs in hunting and horses in racing,

and then they cannot control themselves in larger matters nor cry halt to their contentiousness and ambition.

The most powerful of the Greeks in our time fell to disagreeing first about dancers, then about fiddlers, and from there they began to quarrel about the sites of the baths of Aedipsus and the pavilions and men's halls, and they cut off and diverted the channels, and became so dehumanized and corrupted in the process that their goods were confiscated by a tyrant and they were themselves impoverished and exiled. One might almost say of them that they were now become wholly different men, the only characteristic remaining to them from the past being their hatred of one another. Every effort must therefore be made to resist contentiousness and rivalry, however petty their objects, when they first insinuate themselves between brothers; brothers must accustom themselves to giving ground and yielding the palm, and to taking greater pleasure in being agreeable to their brothers than in winning over them. It was to the fight of the brothers for Thebes that the ancients gave the name "Cadmean victory"—the ugliest and vilest victory of all.

Ah, but do not matters frequently come up which afford occasion for dispute and contention even to people of equable and gentle temper? Indeed they do. But in such cases care must be taken that the dispute be carried on solely on the basis of arguments, without introducing the passions of contentiousness and anger as a goad. Both parties should follow the argument as they would the balances of just scales, and as soon as they have committed the dispute to the verdict of arbitration they should purge it from their minds before it sinks in, like a spot or stain, and becomes ingrained and hard to wash out.

Here we should imitate the Pythagoreans, who had no relationship in blood but only shared a common doctrine: if ever anger drove them to berate one another, before sunset they made their peace and embraced and kissed one another. If an inflammation of the groin is attended by a fever there is no cause for alarm, but if the fever persists after the inflammation has subsided it must be a symptom of illness which has a deeper cause. Just so dissension between brothers which ceases along with the issue between them involves nothing more than the issue; but if the dissension persists then the issue was only a pretext, and its true cause was some deep-seated malady.

It is worth our while to examine a dispute between a pair of barbarian brothers, not about a patch of ground, if you please, nor about slaves or sheep, but about the kingdom of Persia. When Darius died some thought that Ariamenes should be king, for he was the eldest of Darius' sons; others favored Xerxes, whose mother was Atossa daughter of Cyrus, and who was born after Darius attained the kingship. Ariamenes traveled down from the country of the Medes not in military array but peacefully, as for some civil suit. Xerxes, who was on the spot, did all that became a king to do. When his brother arrived he laid aside his diadem, put down the peak of his tiara which regnant kings wear upright, and went out to meet him and gave him cordial welcome. Then he sent him presents, instructing his emissaries to say the following: "With these your brother Xerxes now does you honor. If he shall be declared king by the judgment and the suffrage of the Persians he grants you to stand in second place next after himself." Ariamenes answered: "I accept these presents, but I believe that the kingship of the Persians belongs to me. Yet I shall preserve their honors to my brothers next after my own, and to Xerxes as the first among my brothers."

When the day of judgment arrived the Persians by common consent appointed Artabanus, who was brother of Darius, to be arbiter. Xerxes was reluctant to be judged by him, for he placed great confidence in the crowd, but his mother Atossa reproved him: "Why, my son, do you avoid Artabanus, who is your uncle and the noblest of the Persians? Why are you afraid of a contest in which the second prize is so fair a thing—to be called brother of the king of the Persians?" Xerxes was persuaded, and when the arguments were presented Artabanus' verdict was that the kingship belonged to Xerxes. Ariamenes immediately leapt forward and did obeisance to his brother, and then, taking him by the right hand, seated him upon the royal throne. From that time forth he held the highest place with Xerxes and proved his loyalty to him; at the naval battle of Salamis he distinguished himself and met death for his brother's glory. Let this story stand as an archetype of pure and blameless loyalty and magnanimity.

In the case of Antiochus one might well find fault with his greed for rule, and yet admire him for not wholly extinguishing brotherly love for its sake. For the sake of the kingship he made war against Seleucus; he was the younger brother but had his mother to support his cause. At the height of the war Seleucus joined battle with the Galatians, was defeated, and disappeared from view; it was thought that he was killed when his whole army was cut to pieces by the barbarians. When Antiochus received the news, he laid aside his purple, put on mourning dress, shut the palace, and grieved for his brother. Some time afterwards, when he heard that his brother was safe and had mustered new forces, he came forward to offer sacrifice to the gods and ordered the cities under his rule to offer sacrifice of thanksgiving and wear garlands.

The Athenians devised an absurd myth about strife among the gods, but to this absurdity they joined a quite respectable corrective. The second day of the month Boedromion they always deleted, because the quarrel between Poseidon and Athena was alleged to have taken place on that day. Why should not we too, if ever we have fallen out with our kith and kin, assign that day to oblivion and mark it black on our calendar? Is it not better to forget that one bad day than to forget the many good days when we were brought up and lived together? Either nature's gifts of gentleness and moderation and forebearance for the failings of offspring are vain and useless, or else they must be applied especially to kith and kin. To grant pardon to an offender is no more a valid demonstration of loyalty and affection than for the offender to ask for and receive pardon. Neither, then, should we fall indifferent when tempers are harsh, nor offer resistance when our pardon is begged. When we have wronged another we should frequently forestall his anger by begging his pardon, and again when we have been wronged we should forestall his begging pardon by granting it first.

Euclides the Socratic was much spoken of in the schools for his gentle answer to his brother. When his brother bellowed at him in a raging voice, "I hope to die if I do not get my vengeance on you," Euclides answered, "And I if I do not persuade you to give up your anger and love me as you loved me before." But the thing which King Eumenes did, not merely said, affords an unsurpassable example of gentleness. Perseus, king of the Macedonians, who was his enemy, suborned assassins to murder him, and when they learned that he was going up to Delphi from the sea they set ambush for him near the town, and when he had passed they hurled huge stones down upon his head and neck. He was knocked unconscious and lay apparently dead. News of the event spread abroad everywhere, and certain of Eumenes' friends and servants reached Pergamum, bringing, as they thought, eyewitness accounts of the misfortune. Thereupon Attalus, Eumenes' elder brother, who was a kindly man and most devoted to his brother, was proclaimed king. He not only assumed the crown but married his brother's wife Stratonice and cohabited with her. But then news came that Eumenes was alive and on his way to Pergamum. Attalus laid the diadem aside, put on the guardsman's equipment he had been accustomed to wear, and along with the other guards went to meet Eumenes. Eumenes received him with great kindness and greeted the queen with respect and affection. He lived on for a considerable span, and when he died, without reproach and without suspicion, he bequeathed his kingdom and his wife to Attalus.

And how did Attalus behave? He did not wish to raise up any of his own children, though his wife bore him several after Eumenes died, but educated Eumenes' son, and when he was grown, while he was himself yet alive, placed the diadem upon his head and hailed him king. Cambyses, on the other hand, when he was frightened by a dream that his brother would rule over Asia, took no time for investigation or proof but killed him at once. Thus it came about that when Cambyses died the dynasty of Cyrus was ended and the house of Darius came into power, and Darius was a man who understood how to share his interests and authority not only with his brothers but even with his friends.

Here is another point which must be remembered and carefully observed when a man is at odds with his brothers: at such a time especially he should draw near to and associate with their friends, and avoid and refuse to receive their enemies. In this respect, at least, the practice of the Cretans is to be imitated. Cretans often bicker and fight with each other, but on the approach of an outside enemy they resolve their quarrels and stand together. This is what they themselves call syn-Cretism. There are some people who flow like water into every crack and crevice and subvert familiar friendships; they hate both alike but direct their attack against the one whose weakness makes him susceptible to it.

When a man is in love his ingenuous and innocent friends support his passion; but when a man is angry and at odds with his brother, then the most malignant of his enemies seem to join in his indignation and his rage. The proper response is that made by the hen to the cat in Aesop's fable. When the cat, with pretended solicitude, inquired of the ailing hen how she did, the hen answered, "Very well, if only you would go away." So should one say to the sort of man who brings the quarrel up in conversation and asks questions and burrows after secrets: "I have no quarrel at all with my brother if neither I nor he pay any attention to slanderers." When people's eyes are infected we recommend that they turn their sight towards colors and objects which do not produce an injurious reflection; I cannot understand why it is that in cases of fault-finding and anger and suspicion towards our brothers we take such pleasure in forming close alliances with people who will aggravate our trouble. It would be far better to run from hateful and malicious people, to approach our brothers' connections and familiars and friends, to discuss the grievances in frank conversations with their wives. They say that when brothers walk together they ought not let a stone come between them on the road; they are distressed if even a dog run between them, and they observe many similar scruples which have nothing to do with disturbing brotherly harmony. But they cannot see that they are permitting doggish men whose slanders do work mischief to come between them.

Hence (the course of the discussion itself suggests this point) we applaud the saying of Theophrastus: "If friends hold their goods in common, friends in particular should be held in common by friends." This admonition is particularly applicable to brothers. Separate and individual associations and intimacies direct them away from one another and estrange them from each other. If they are fond of different people it follows that they find pleasure in different pursuits, emulate different characters, and are influenced by different guides. Friendships shape character, and there is no plainer sign of diversity of character than the choice of diverse friends. It follows that neither eating and drinking together, neither playing nor passing time together, is so close a bond of concord as sharing the same inclinations and revulsions, as taking pleasure in the same society or again loathing and avoiding it. Common friendships leave no room for calumny and conflict. Even if any anger or reproach arises it is dissolved by the mediation of friends, who take it upon themselves to disperse it if they are intimate with both parties and are inclined towards both with the same benevolence. Just as fragments of bronze are fitted together and joined by a solder of tin which touches the edge of each fragment and accommodates itself to the temper of each, so ought a friend be accommodating to both brothers in common and weld their good will in a close bond. But those who are not evenly modulated, like discordant notes in a musical composition, produce not union but cleavage. We may therefore question whether Hesiod was right or wrong when he said [*Works and Days* 707], "Do not make your comrade equal with your brother." A right-minded friend who is shared by both, as has been said, or rather modulated to both, is a bond of brotherly love. But Hesiod seems to have been apprehensive of the vulgar majority because of their greed and self-seeking. But if one is on guard against these evils a friend may indeed be treated as a brother.

But even if a man holds a friend in equal esteem with a brother he should be careful to assign his brother precedence in magistracies and public offices, in invitations and introductions to important personages; in all things which enhance distinction and increase reputation in the sight of the crowd it is proper to render nature its due status of dignity. In these matters giving preference to a friend does not so enhance his dignity as a slight disgraces and diminishes the reputation of a brother. But opinions on this subject are recorded at length elsewhere. The saying of Menander, "No lover willingly sees himself neglected," is quite right. It admonishes and teaches us to be attentive to our brothers and not, in our reliance on nature, to neglect them. Horses are naturally attached to humans and dogs love their masters, but if they do not receive care and attention they lose their affection and become estranged; the body is most closely attached to the soul, but if it is not cared for by the soul and neglected it refuses to cooperate with the soul and deserts and spoils its works.

It is a fine thing to show attention to brothers, and even better to show attention to their fathers-in-law and brothers-in-law and a kindly and eager interest in all that pertains to them; one should give affectionate greetings to servants who love their masters and be grateful to physicians who have cured them and to faithful friends who have been their comrades in travel and military service abroad. A brother's wife one should respect and revere as the holiest of sanctities; one should esteem and bless her for her husband's sake, share her distress when she is neglected, and mollify her when she is irritated. If she has committed some minor offense one should help reconcile and placate her husband. And if a man have any private difference with his brother he should make his complaint to the wife and resolve the difficulty with her. He should be most concerned if his brother is unmarried and childless, and by encouragement and reproof sway him to marry and to undertake the customary obligations of matrimony. And when his brother has gotten children he should manifest even greater affection for him and respect for his wife.

He should be as well disposed to his brother's children as to his own, and even kindlier and more indulgent. Then if they commit such faults as young people do they will not in their fear run from their father and mother and take recourse to bad and foolish companions, but will have a shelter and refuge along with kindly admonition and intercession. So Plato reclaimed his nephew Speusippus from sloth and debauchery without saying or doing a disagreeable word or deed. The young man had run away from his parents who were always berating and reproaching him, and by showing himself calm and passionless Plato aroused him not only to a sense of shame but also to emulation of himself and his philosophy. Many of Plato's friends chided him for not admonishing the lad, but he said that he did indeed admonish him in that his own life and habits provided a lesson in distinguishing between the honorable and the base.

The father of Aleuas the Thessalian kept him under strict curb and was severe with him because he was high-handed and willful, but his uncle received him and won him over. When the Thessalians sent roast beans to the oracle at Delphi as lots for selecting their king, the uncle, unbeknownst to Aleuas' father, inserted one bean bearing Aleuas' name. When the Pythia selected that bean the father declared that he had put none in for his son, and everyone thought there had been some mistake in writing down the names. They therefore sent to inquire of the oracle a second time, and the Pythia by way of confirming her first utterance said, "The red-haired lad I mean, whom Archedice bore." And in this manner was Aleuas designated king by Apollo through his father's brother, and he himself far surpassed his predecessors and advanced his race to great glory and power.

Verily, a man ought to rejoice in the achievements and distinctions and preferments of his brother's children, and by exalting them enlarge their spirit and so spur them on to higher excellence, and praise them unstintingly when they succeed. For a man to sing the praises of his own son may be invidious, but to praise his brother's is splendid; it denotes not love of self but love of excellence, and is truly divine. It seems to me that the very title of uncle [*theios*, which also means "divine"] suggests benevolent love to nephews. We must emulate the conduct of divine beings. Heracles begot sixty-eight sons, but loved his nephews as well as any of them. To this day his nephew Iolaus shares a common altar with him and they are invoked in prayer together, Iolaus under the designation "Heracles' comrade." When Heracles' brother Iphicles was killed in battle in Lacedaemonia Heracles was smitten with grief and left all the Peloponnese behind him. Leucothea nursed her sister's infant when her sister died, and deified the child along with herself. That is why the Roman matrons at the festival of Leucothea (whom they call Matuta) embrace and show honor not to their own children but to their sisters'.

Marriage Counsel

This is a wedding present to his disciples Pollianus and Eurydice in which Plutarch summarizes in brief the doctrines he had previously imparted to them at length. It contains 48 short paragraphs of stories and parables calculated to deepen the bridal couple's understanding of, and appreciation for, one another and the conjugal state. The emphasis is on consideration, spiritual awareness, and reasonableness. The bride is urged to cultivate her intellect and eschew frivolity and excessive adornment, but she must not allow herself to become a bluestocking or dowdy.

I SEND YOU, dear Pollianus and Eurydice, my best wishes. Like the traditional ritual which the priestess of Demeter performed for you when you were shut into your bridal chamber, the subjoined discourse is applicable to both of you alike and will be a contribution to your hymeneal chants. I hope that it will be found useful and in accord with our usages.

In music there is a mode for the flute called the Rearing Horse. It appears to arouse stallions to heat and facilitate their coupling. In the numerous and excellent themes of philosophy there is none more worthy of study than that which deals with marriage, for it binds those who have joined together to share their lives into oneness and renders them considerate and tractable to one another. These things you have often heard, for you were nurtured in a philosophic environment; but to make them easier to remember I have arranged the principal points in a series of brief parables. These I send to you both as a gift, and I pray that the Muses attend and collaborate with Aphrodite, for I believe that it is no greater part of their office to provide that lyre or zither is well attuned than it is to render marriage and the household the same service through discourse and harmony and philosophy. To signify that the pleasures of marriage have need of discourse, the ancients gave Hermes a place beside Aphrodite; and there they placed Persuasion and the Graces also, so that husband and wife might obtain their desires of one another by persuasion and not by contention and bickering.

Solon directed that the bride should munch a quince before lying down beside the groom, probably to intimate that the grace of mouth and voice should be harmonious and sweet from the beginning.

In Boeotia, after veiling the bride they crown her with asparagus. Just as asparagus produces very agreeable fruit from very prickly thorns, so the bride will provide gentle and sweet companionship if the groom does not withdraw in vexation at her initial asperity. Those who will not abide the petulance of a young girl are no different from those who abandon a vine to others because the grapes are unripe. Many newly married women, on the other hand, are annoyed with a husband because of his early behavior; their experience is like that of a man who endures the sting of the bee and then abandons its honey.

Especially in the beginning should newly married couples guard against disagreements and friction; they should observe that vessels made of joined parts are at first easily pulled apart by any chance pretext, but when time has welded the joints fast they can hardly be loosened by fire and steel.

Just as fire kindles easily in chaff and strands and hare's wool but is quickly extinguished unless it catches some other material able to retain and feed it, so the sharp passion of newlyweds which flares up because of bodily attraction must not be regarded as enduring or constant unless it attains a viable condition by being based upon character and attracted to reason.

Fishing with poison is a quick and easy way to lure and take a fish, but makes it bad and inedible. Similarly women who contrive philters and sorceries for their husbands and make them docile through lasciviousness find themselves married to brain-struck and degenerate fools. The men Circe drugged were of no profit to her; she made no use of them when they turned into swine and asses. But

Odysseus, who retained his wits and was intelligent company, she loved exceedingly.

Women who would rather rule over fools than listen to sensible men are like those who would rather guide the blind than follow those who know the road and can see.

Women will not believe that Pasiphae, who was married to a king, fell in love with a bull, and yet they can see that some women are chafed by austere and prudent men and prefer to cohabit with those compounded of licentiousness and sensuality, like dogs or goats.

Men who cannot leap into the saddle for want of strength or vigor teach their horses to kneel and crouch down. Similarly some men who have got well-born and rich wives do not improve themselves but humble their wives, the better to rule them when they have become lowly. But just as a man ought to consider the stature of a horse when using the bridle, so ought he regard the dignity of a wife.

The moon, when it is at a distance from the sun, is conspicuous and luminous to our sight, but when she is near the sun she hides herself and disappears. With a virtuous woman the situation is reversed: she should be visible when she is with her husband, and keep to her house and hide when she is not.

Herodotus' remark [1.8] that "a woman takes off her modesty when she takes off her clothing" is wrong. The contrary is true: a virtuous woman puts on modesty instead, and husband and wife understand that great modesty is a token of great love.

Two notes may be sounded in harmony, but the melody is carried by the deeper voice: so every activity in a virtuous household is carried on by husband and wife in harmony, but the guidance and decision of the husband is apparent.

The sun overcame the north wind. The wind tried to strip a man of his cloak perforce, but the stiffer he blew the closer the man wrapped his cloak about him and the tighter he grasped its skirt. But after the wind came the heat of the sun. The man grew warm and then hot, and removed not only his cloak but his tunic also. Many women behave similarly. When their husbands try to curb their luxury and extravagance perforce they grow angry and resist, but with the persuasions of reason they lay such things aside amicably and practice moderation.

Cato ejected a man from the senate for kissing his own wife in the presence of his daughter. Perhaps this was too censorious. But it is indecent for people to caress and kiss and embrace each other in the presence of others. Surely, then, it is more indecent to scold and bicker in the presence of others. If a man's intimacies and tenderness to his wife should be in private, surely his correction and fault-finding and reproaches should not be spread abroad in public.

A mirror that does not reflect a true likeness is of no use even though it is embellished with gold and precious stones, and similarly a rich wife is of no use if she does not conform her life to her husband's and harmonize her character with his. If a mirror returns a gloomy likeness of a cheerful man, or a cheerful and smiling likeness of a sad and scowling man, it is false and worthless. Similarly a wife is worthless and perverse if she puts on a scowling expression when her husband has an impulse to be playful and tender, and is playful and mirthful when he is serious. The former suggests sourness, and the latter contempt. Lines and planes, as they say in geometry, have no motion of their own, but move as bodies move; so a woman ought have no private emotions but share with her husband in seriousness and in playfulness, in thoughtfulness and in mirth.

Men who do not like to see their wives eat with them only teach them to stuff themselves when they are alone. Similarly those who are not cheerful in the company of their wives and do not share with them in playfulness and mirth are only teaching them to seek their own pleasures apart from their husbands.

The Persian kings have their lawful wives sit with them at dinner and feast with them. But when the kings wish to be sportive and get drunk they send their wives away and call in music girls and concubines. This procedure is correct, for it prevents wives from participating in debauchery and drunkenness. Hence if a private individual who is prone to incontinent indulgence transgresses with a courtesan or servant girl his wife ought not to be vexed or cross but rather to reflect that it is respect for her that makes him choose another outlet for his drunkenness and incontinence and wantonness.

Kings devoted to music make many musicians, those devoted to scholarship many scholars, those devoted to athletics many athletes. So a husband devoted to his personal appearance makes his wife a prinker, one devoted to pleasure makes her a wanton voluptuary, but one devoted to what is good and fair makes her prudent and decent.

A Spartan lass was asked whether she had ever approached a man. "No," she answered, "but a man has approached me." Such behavior, I take it, is appropriate for a housewife, neither to avoid such relationship or be vexed when her husband takes the initiative, nor yet to take the initiative herself; for the one course is lascivious and brazen, the other haughty and unamiable.

A wife ought not to acquire friends of her own, but share in her husband's friends. First and greatest of friends are the gods, and hence it becomes the wife to worship the gods her husband believes in and to recognize none other. Her house door should be closed to exotic rites and alien superstitions. No god can be pleased with clandestine and surreptitious rituals performed by a woman.

"That state is prosperous and happy," says Plato [*Republic* 462c], "in which Mine and Thine are seldom uttered and heard, for then the citizens treat everything worth attention as common property, so far as practicable." So much the more then should such expressions be banished from the married state. Physicians declare that blows on the left side of the body affect the reactions on the right: so it is well for the wife to share in her husband's reactions and the husband in his wife's. Thus the community of interest is preserved by their joint contributions, each reciprocating the other's good will, just as cables receive strength from one another by being intertwined. Nature joins our bodies in an amalgam, taking a portion from each and blending it to produce offspring common to both, so that neither can distinguish or define his own or the other's part. In property too the same partnership should obtain among married couples. They should pool and combine all their possessions into a single holding, and neither should regard this portion as his and that as the other's, but each should regard the whole as his and no portion the other's. And just as we call a blend "wine" though the greater proportion is water, so the property and household should be referred to as the husband's, even though the wife may have contributed the larger share.

Helen loved wealth, Paris pleasure; Odysseus was prudent and Penelope chaste. The marriage of the latter was blessed and enviable, while that of the former produced an Iliad of woes for Greeks and barbarians.

The Roman who was admonished by his friends for having put away a wife who was virtuous and rich and beautiful, held his shoe up and said: "This too is beautiful to the sight and new, but no one knows where it pinches me." It is not in her dowry, then, nor on her birth or beauty that a woman ought to trust but on the qualities which give her a particular hold on her husband—comradeship and character and community of interest. The former factors produce hardness and vexation day by day, the latter harmony and tranquillity and affection. Physicians are more apprehensive of fevers which arise from obscure causes and increase gradually than of those which have an obvious and tangible explanation. So it is the slight frictions which pass unnoticed by the majority but which are continuous and unremitting that set man and wife at odds and sicken their married life.

King Philip fell in love with a Thessalian woman. She was charged with using magic charms upon him, and [his wife] Olympias was eager to get the creature into her power. But when she came into the queen's presence she proved to be comely and her conversation genteel and sensible. "Away with these calumnies!" said Olympias, "The charms you have are in yourself." A thing irresistible, then, is a lawfully wedded wife who includes all advantages in her own disposition—dowry and birth and magic charms and even Aphrodite's girdle—and thus achieves the affection of her husband by character and merit.

This same Olympias remarked, when a young courtier married a handsome woman whose reputation was bad, "That fellow has no mind, else he would never have married for his eyes." But a man ought no more marry for his fingers than for his eyes—as some do who reckon up how much a woman brings with her rather than judge how she would be to live with.

This is how Socrates admonished young men who looked at mirrors: the ugly he bade correct their defect by virtue, and the handsome not to disgrace their beauty by baseness. For a matron too it is a good practice to talk to herself when she has mirror in hand. The homely one should say, "How [bad] if I were not virtuous!" And the beauty, "How [good] if I am virtuous as well?" It is a high distinction for a homely woman to be loved for her character rather than for beauty.

The tyrant of Sicily sent expensive clothing and jewelry to Lysander's daughters, but Lysander refused to accept them. Said he: "This finery will rather disgrace my daughters than adorn them." But before Lysander's time Sophocles had said: "Not adornment, you wretch, but its reverse would the frenzy of your heart display." Here is Crates' definition: "Adornment is what adorns." What adorns a woman is what enhances her comeliness. This is achieved not by gold or emeralds or scarlet but by whatever enhances her dignity, her decency, her propriety.

When sacrifice is offered to Hera as patroness of wedlock the gall is not consecrated with the rest of the offering but removed and cast out beside the altar: by this usage the lawgiver implied that no gall, or anger, should be present in a marriage. A matron's tartness ought to be wholesome and agreeable, like wine's, not bitter, like aloes or medicines.

Plato advised Xenocrates, who was of somewhat coarse temperament but otherwise a gentleman, to offer sacrifice to the Graces. In my judgment the virtuous woman in particular has need of the Graces so that, as Metrodorus puts it, "she may lead an agreeable life with her husband and not be irate because she is chaste." The devoted wife should no more neglect affection than the frugal wife cleanliness, for asperity makes propriety as disagreeable as slovenliness makes simplicity.

A woman who refrains from laughing with her husband or joking with him for fear she may appear bold and wanton is no different from one who will not put oil on her hair for fear she may be thought to use perfume and not wash her face for fear she be thought to use rouge. Some poets and orators carefully avoid vulgarity and meanness and preciosity in their expressions, but we observe that they do use every art to sway and stir their public by their subject matter, and by their arrangement and lifelike treatment of it. Similarly a matron precisely because she avoids and deprecates all that is excessive, seductive, and ostentatious, as indeed she should, ought all the more use every art of character and gracious habits to accustom her husband to life with her that is desirable because it is agreeable. But if a wife's nature prove austere, uncompromising, and moody, the husband must be patient. Phocion, when Antipater enjoined upon him a course which was neither honorable nor decent, declared, "You cannot use me both as friend and flatterer." So a husband should reason about a virtuous but austere wife, "I cannot have her both as wife and mistress."

Egyptian women were not permitted, according to traditional custom, to wear shoes, so that they should keep to their houses all the time. Most women, if you take their gilt shoes away, their bracelets, anklets, purple, and pearls, stay at home.

Theano bared her arm as she put on her cloak, and someone remarked, "What a beautiful arm!" "But it is not public," Theano said. Not only must the arm of a virtuous woman not be public, but neither should her speech. She should be as observant and guarded in exposing her voice as her person before strangers, for her speech reveals her emotions and character and temper.

Phidias fashioned the Aphrodite of the Eleans treading upon a tortoise, to symbolize keeping home and silence for women. A woman's talk should be to her husband or through her husband, nor ought she take it amiss if, like a flautist, she produces a more impressive note through another's tongue.

Rich men and kings when they bestow honor on philosophers, adorn themselves as well as the philosophers; but philosophers who court the rich do not add to the reputation of the rich but only diminish their own. So it happens in the case of women. If they subordinate themselves to their husbands they win praise, but if they wish to dominate they are more absurd than their subjects. But though the husband should dominate over the wife, his domination should not be that of an owner over a chattel, but that of the soul over the body; he should enter into her feelings and be grafted into her nature through good will.

Philosophers distinguish unions of bodies into several classes: some consist of disparate members, like an army or navy; some of members fitted together, like a house or ship; and some of members welded and grafted together, like any living creature. The case of marriage is analogous: those who marry for love are welded and grafted together; those who marry for dowry or procreation are fitted together; but the marriage of persons who merely sleep together consists of disparate members of whom one might say that they dwell rather than live together. Physicists say that a mixture of liquids implies a consistent combination throughout; so a marriage should be a mutual amalgam of bodies and property and friends and relations. So the Roman lawgiver forbade spouses to give or receive gifts from one another, not in order to prevent their sharing but rather that they might regard all their possessions as common.

At Leptis, a city in Libya, it is traditional for the bride, on the day after the marriage, to send to the groom's mother and ask for a pot. The groom's mother refuses and says she has no pot, in order that from the very outset the bride may understand that the mother-in-law's character is that of a stepmother, so that if any friction arises subsequently she may not be angry or resentful. A wife ought to recognize this hostility and cure its cause, which is the mother's jealousy of her son's affection for his wife. The sole cure of this indisposition is to promote her husband's affection for herself without relaxing or diminishing his affection for his mother.

Mothers appear to love their sons better because their sons are able to help them, and fathers their daughters, because their daughters require their help. Another reason may be that parents honor each other, and each wishes to manifest his appreciation and affection for the qualities characteristic of the other. There may be exceptions, but it is an intelligent thing for the wife to show respect to her husband's parents rather than look to her own, and in case of any distress to resort to them and say nothing to her own parents. Evidence of trust begets trust, and love is reciprocated by love.

The Greeks in Cyrus' army were ordered by their generals to receive the attack in silence if the enemy charged with a shout, but if the enemy were silent to charge with a shout. Women of sense hold their peace when their husbands raise their voices in temper, but when their husbands fall silent they talk to them and soothe them with words of comfort.

Euripides reproves those who play the lyre over their wine. And rightly so, for music ought to be invited to assuage passion and sorrow rather than to increase the titillation of pleasure. So you must be assured of the error of people who lie down together for the sake of pleasure but sleep apart when they fall into angry disagreement. That is just the time for them to invoke Aphrodite, who is the best physician for such cases. Such, we may say, is the prescription of the poet [Homer] who represents Hera as saying: "Their unsettled quarrels will I resolve, and send them to their bed to be united in endearment."

Always and everywhere a wife ought to avoid clashing with her husband and a husband with his wife, but they ought particularly to guard against clashes when they go to rest together and sleep together. When her attendants sought to prevail upon a woman in the throes of travail to take to her bed, she said, "How can bed cure the ailment I contracted in bed?" But the disagreements and reproaches and vexations which bed begets cannot easily be composed in any other time and place.

The remark of Hermione [in Euripides' *Andromache*] seems to be just: " 'Twas the visits of evil women that destroyed me." But such a result is not automatic: it is only when they have been at odds with their husbands and jealous that a wife's ears, let alone her doors, are open to such women. It is at such times in particular that a sensible wife should stop her ears and beware of whispers, so that fire should not be added to fire. There is a saying of Philip's she should keep ready to hand. When his friends were in-stigating Philip against the Greeks on the grounds that though he treated them well they spoke ill of him, he is said to have replied, "What would they do if I treated them ill?" So when the gossips say, "You love your husband and are virtuous and yet he treats you badly," the wife should answer, "What would he do if I should begin to hate and wrong him?"

A man whose slave had run away caught sight of the culprit, after an interval of time, and gave chase. The fleeing slave darted into a treadmill for refuge, whereupon the man said, "Is there any situation I would rather find you in?" Similarly a woman who is angry with her husband and suing him for divorce because of jealousy should say to herself, "Is there any situation my rival would rather find me in than being angry with my husband and suing him and deserting my home and bed?"

Ritual plowing is celebrated by the Athenians thrice: first at Scirum, to commemorate the most ancient sowing of all; next at Raria; and third the so-called Buzygius, under the Acropolis. But more sacred than all of these is the marital sowing and plowing for the procreation of children. Sophocles' "Cytherea of fair fruits" is a beautiful epithet for Aphrodite. Therefore should man and wife use this sowing with particular circumspection. They should keep themselves unsullied by unholy and unlawful inter-course with others, nor sow seed they do not wish to burgeon into fruit and would so embarrass them, if it came to birth, that they would be ashamed and keep it hidden.

When the orator Gorgias recited his discourse on

harmony to the Greeks assembled at Olympia, Melanthus remarked: "This man is offering advice about concord, and he cannot prevail upon himself, his wife, and his maid, three persons in all, to live in concord." It seems that the girl was an object of Gorgias' love and his wife's jealousy. A man who sets about introducing harmony into a city or assembly or among friends must first have his own household well harmonized. The majority of people is much more likely to notice a man's offenses against his wife than it is to notice her offenses.

Cats are said to be excited to a state of frenzy by the odor of perfumes. If it were the case that women were similarly deranged and made savage by perfumes, it would be monstrous for their husbands not to abstain from perfume and be indifferent to their wives' misery for the sake of their own transitory pleasure. But, since women are so affected by husbands who resort not to perfume but to courtesans, it is unjust for husbands so to grieve and distress their wives for the sake of brief pleasure. They should approach their wives pure and unsullied by intercourse with other women as they do bees, (who are said to be incensed with and attack men who have consorted with women).

Elephants should not be approached by a man dressed in white nor bulls by one dressed in red, for the beasts are made savage by these colors. Tigers are said to go mad altogether when they are surrounded by tambourines and tear themselves to pieces. Among men, too, some cannot tolerate the sight of scarlet and purple clothing and others loathe cymbals and tambourines. Is it so dreadful for wives to abstain from these things and not irritate and embitter their husbands but rather to be at one with them with consideration and mildness?

When Philip was trying to force a woman against her will she said to him, "Let me go. All women are alike when the light is out." This is an excellent answer to adulterers and licentious men, but a married woman ought not be like any chance female when the light is out. It is when her body is invisible that her virtue and her sole devotion and affection for her husband should be evident.

Plato [*Laws* 729c] used to admonish older men in particular to "be shamefast before the young," so that the young might behave decently before them. "Where the old are shameless," he thought, "the young cannot acquire modesty or circumspection." This a husband ought to bear in mind; to no one should he show greater respect than to his wife, for to her their chamber must become a school of orderliness or of wantonness. But a man who keeps his wife from the pleasures which he himself enjoys is no whit different from one who bids his wife fight to the death against enemies to whom he has himself capitulated.

On the question of love of finery, my dear Eurydice, do read and try to remember what [my wife] Timoxena wrote to Aristylla. And for your part, my dear Pollianus, do not imagine that your wife will refrain from excess and extravagance if she observes that you do not despise these tendencies in others but yourself take pleasure in the gilt of cups, wall paintings in rooms, trapping of mules, and ornaments on horses' necks. It is not possible to expel from the women's apartment the luxury which has easy entree in the men's. You are now at a time of life suitable for philosophy: adorn your character, then, with thorough and logically reasoned treatises, and find and attend upon teachers who will benefit you. The useful things you collect you must bring to your wife, collecting, as the bees do, from various sources and carrying it in your own person. Deliver your store to her and discuss it with her, and make the choicest portions her favorite and familiar doctrine. [In Homer Andromache says to her husband:] "Thou art father to me and dear mother, yea, and brother too." It is no less lofty for a man to hear his wife say, "Thou art guide to me and philosopher, yea, and teacher of what is excellent and divine." The first advantage of such studies is that they divert women from trivialities. A woman who has learned geometry will be ashamed to dance, and she will not invite the enchantments of magic if she is enchanted by the discourses of Plato and Xenophon. And if any claim power to pull down the moon she will laugh at the ignorance and folly of women who believe such things, for she herself has had lessons in astronomy and is familiar with the story of Aglaonice, daughter of Hegetor the Thessalian. Aglaonice was well informed about eclipses of the full moon and knew in advance when the moon was due to be overtaken by the earth's shadow: she therefore deceived the women into believing that she herself was pulling the moon down.

No child was ever born of a woman, it is said, without the participation of a man; yet in a woman's womb there do occur amorphous, fleshy growths which take on hardness out of their own corruption and are called *mylai*. That such growths find no place in a woman's soul the greatest of care must be exercised. If they do not receive the seed of good doctrine, if they do not participate with their husband in cultural interests, then they become pregnant with monstrous growths of worthless notions and passions.

For your part, Eurydice, make a special effort to maintain familiarity with the utterances of wise and good men and to keep ever on your lips those sayings which you learned from us when you were a girl. So you will afford your husband joy, and your extraordinary and noble adornment, for which there is nothing to pay, will be admired by other women. One rich lady's precious pearls and another's foreign silks you cannot acquire or put on unless you buy them at a high price, but without charge you may wear the adornments of Theano, Cleobulina, Gorgo wife of Leonidas, Timoclea sister of Theagenes, the ancient Claudia, Cornelia daughter of Scipio, and all the other women who have been admired and famous. Attired in these you may live a life at once reputable and happy. Sappho regarded her own exquisite compositions with sufficient confidence to write to a certain rich woman: "Thou shalt die and lie buried, and no memory of thee shall survive, for share in the roses of Pieria thou hast none." Surely you have better right to proud and shining self-esteem if you have a share not only in the roses but also in the fruit which the Muses bring and vouchsafe to those who esteem culture and philosophy.

Consolation to His Wife

The Consolation was a well-established literary form in later antiquity. The best-known of the surviving specimens are Seneca's polished consolations *To Helvia, To Marcia,* and *To Polybius.* The present example is far more attractive and more moving because of its genuineness. It may have been edited for publication but the circumstances of its composition are surely as Plutarch states them. The fact that the only literary allusions are quotations from Euripides and Theognis and an Aesopic fable, all of which Plutarch surely carried in his head, shows that the piece was actually written away from his study. Near as Plutarch comes to Christian ethics he is characteristically pagan in his belief in man's natural goodness. Little Timoxena was naturally good and eager to share her treasures with her friends; if she had lived to grow up the pressure of life might have made her less good. The well-fed infant in St. Augustine's *Confessions* who would not let his mother nurse a starving stranger was naturally depraved and would require outside pressure to redeem him.

M^Y DEAR WIFE:

The messenger you sent with tidings of the death of our little daughter apparently missed me on his road to Athens, and consequently I learned about the child only when I arrived in Tanagra. I suppose that the funeral has already taken place. I could wish that the arrangements were such as to cause you the minimum of pain, both for the present and the future. If you have omitted any ceremony which you think might lighten your grief because you wished to await my approval, do carry it out. But excesses and superstitions should be avoided; I know it is not in your character to indulge in them.

Above all, my dear wife, help us both preserve our customary composure in this affliction. I am of course very sensible of it and feel its force; but if I find your grief exceeds due measure I shall be more greatly distressed than by the misfortune itself. Neither am I "fashioned of oak or stone," as is well known to you, who have shared with me in the nurture of our several children, all of whom we have ourselves brought up at home.

After the birth of our four sons you yearned for a daughter, and I seized the opportunity of giving her your dear name: I know that she was precious to you. Peculiar poignancy attaches to tenderness for children when their presence is altogether welcome and completely untainted by ill will and reproach. The child herself possessed a marvelous cheeriness of temper and gentleness, and her responsiveness to love and eagerness to please evoked not only pleasure but an appreciation of human goodness. She would invite her nurse to offer her breast not only to other infants but even to furnishings and toys in which she took delight. It was as if, out of humane sensibilities, she invited them to her own table, to share in the good things she had; what was most delightful to her she wished all who pleased her to enjoy.

I cannot see, my dear wife, why these and similar qualities which delighted us when she was alive should now distress and confound us when we bring them to mind. Rather do I fear lest we lose those memories along with our grief, like that Clymene who said, "I hate that well-turned cornel bow; away with all exercises!" She avoided and shuddered at every reminder of her son. In general, nature avoids everything that causes distress. But in the case of our child, in the degree that she proved to us a thing most lovable to fondle and look at and hear, so the memory of her must abide with us and become part of us, and it will bring us a greater quantity and variety of joy than of sorrow. Surely some portion of the discourses I have uttered to others should prove helpful to ourselves in time of need; we must not then sink into lethargy nor conjure up the sorrows which are the price of those numerous delights.

I was told by those who were present and found your conduct remarkable that you did not put on mourning nor induce any uncomeliness or unseemliness in yourself or in your servants, that there was no preparation for extravagant solemnities at the grave, but that everything was done decently and quietly with only the family in attendance. For my part I was not surprised, for you would never prink for the theater or processions, but even for pleasurable outings thought that extravagance was useless and maintained your sensible moderation even among people who looked askance at it. It is not only in bacchic celebrations that a virtuous woman must remain uncorrupted, but in sorrow too she must remember that excess is to be avoided and that transports of emotion require to be controlled; it is not her love, as the many think, that she must fight against, but the incontinence of her soul. Upon love we bestow sorrow and respect and an abiding memory of the departed; but the insatiable yearning for lamentation which leads to wailing and beating of the breast is no less shameful than unbridled voluptuousness—though men find it venial, for it is a bitter smart rather than an agreeable sensation which is associated with the impropriety. What could be more illogical than to check excess of laughter and gaiety and then give free flow to rivers of tears and lamentations which stream from the same source? Or, as some husbands do, to quarrel with their wives over the use of perfumery and purple and then suffer them to shear their hair in mourning, to dye their garments black, to sit in unnatural attitudes and recline in uncomfortable postures? Or, what is hardest of all, to oppose their wives and prevent them if they chastise their servants or maids immoderately or unfairly, and then to overlook it when they chastise themselves unfeelingly and cruelly in trying circumstances which call for gentleness and kindliness?

But between us, my dear wife, there was never any occasion for such differences, nor, I think, will there ever be. The simplicity of your grooming and the frugality of your diet has evoked the astonishment of all the philosophers who have ever visited or associated with us. Nor is there any of our townsmen who has not remarked upon your admirable simplicity at festivals and sacrifices and theatrical performances. Upon a similar occasion in the past you demonstrated your singular steadfastness when you lost the eldest of your children; and it was the same when charming Charon left us. I remember that friends were escorting me on my way from the seashore when the news of my son's death was brought, and they together with others accompanied me to the house. When they observed perfect orderliness and quiet in the house they thought, as they afterwards confided in others, that nothing amiss had happened and that it was an empty rumor that reached me. So discreetly had you arranged your household at a juncture which offered occasion for great disorder. And yet you yourself suckled that son, and underwent surgery when your breast suffered a contusion. That is the conduct of a noble woman and a loving mother.

The majority of mothers, we observe, take their children into their arms, when others have bathed them and prinked them out, and treat them like dolls; and then, if the children die, they dissolve into empty and ungrateful grief, not out of affection, for affection is rational and dignified; but vainglory mixed with a modicum of natural feeling produces wild and unassuageable transports of grief. This phenomenon Aesop understood very well. When Zeus distributed their honors to the gods, he tells us, Grief too put in a request, and Zeus ordained that Grief should indeed receive honor, but only from those who elected and desired to bestow it. This is exactly what happens. In the beginning everyone welcomes Grief into his house, and then when it has had time to take root and has become a companion and housemate it will no longer depart when the inmates wish it to. It must therefore be resisted at the threshold and not be allowed within the citadel by way of mourning dress or shorn locks or other such tokens, which, confronting and glowering upon us daily, render our spirit petty and narrow and confined and unsmiling and timorous, so that it has no share in jollity or brightness or the kindly board, being so besieged and hard pressed by grief. Upon this evil there follows neglect of the body and aversion to anointing, bathing, and other attention to the person. The opposite should be the case; a troubled soul should itself receive support from a robust body. A great part of sorrow is blunted and relaxed, like a wave under a clear sky, when the body enjoys tranquil sailing. But where a bad regimen begets meagerness and roughness and the body transmits nothing that is beneficial or salutary to the soul but only pain and discomfort, like acrid and annoying exhalations, then it can no longer easily recover even if it wish to do so. Such are the afflictions which visit a soul that has been thus abused.

But the dreadful thing which does so much mischief in these cases I need have no fear of—I mean the visits of silly women and their cries and the continuing lamentations by which they fan and whet grief and prevent it from abating either through other causes or of itself. I know the good fight you lately fought when you supported Theon's sister and resisted the women who were charging in with wails and shrieks, simply to pile fire upon fire. When people see a friend's house aflame they extinguish it with all possible speed and strength, but when souls are ablaze they only add kindling. When a man's eyes are sore his friends do not let him finger them, however much he wishes to, nor do they themselves touch the inflammation. But a man sunk in grief suffers every chance comer to stir and augment his affliction, like a running sore; and by reason of the fingering and consequent irritation it hardens into a serious and intractable evil. Against such a contingency I know that you will be on guard.

Endeavor often to transpose yourself in imagination to the period when our child was not yet born, and yet we had no cause to reproach fortune; and then consider that our present state is a continuation of that former period, for our condition is now as it was then. If we look upon our situation in the past as freer of reproach than our present state we shall seem to be resentful that our child was ever born. The two years of her life that intervened must by no means be effaced from our memory but rathered reckoned as a pleasure, for they afforded us delight and happiness. We must never consider a small good as a large evil, nor be ungrateful for what fortune has given us because it has not filled the measure as full as we expected. Always respectfulness to the divine and a

cheerful and uncomplaining attitude towards fortune produces fruit that is good and sweet. In case of misfortune
there is no surer means of either quenching grief entirely
or diminishing its size and intensity by an admixture of
opposite emotions than by calling to mind good things in
the past and transposing and reshaping our reflections
upon life from the gloomy and troubled to the bright and
shining. Perfumes not only delight our sense of smell
but are an antidote to bad odors. Similarly, recollection
of good things in the midst of evil functions as a necessary
remedy for such as do not avoid the memory of past blessings and do not always and everywhere upbraid fortune.
It becomes us ill, inculpating our own lives, to find fault
with a single blot, as in a book, when all the rest is clean
and unstained.

You have oftentimes heard that happiness depends
upon a correct rationale which renders a temperament
steadfast, and that changes of fortune do not produce
significant deviations and contribute no great weight to
the direction our lives take. But even if we allow ourselves
to be governed, like the majority, by external events and
take into our reckoning the untoward strokes of fortune,
and if we gauge our happiness by the judgment of ordinary
folk, still I must caution you to take no account of the
tears and lamentations of visitors who follow the tiresome
custom of paying condolence calls. Rather reflect how
much these people envy you for your children, your household, your way of life. It would be a perversity for you
to find fault with your estate and chafe at it when others
would cheerfully choose your lot even with the affliction
which now distresses us. Nay, this present sting should
make you sensible of our numerous blessings which remain
untouched. Shall we imitate those who collect Homeric
lines which are defective at beginning or end and overlook
large and excellent stretches of his poetry? Shall we metic-
ulously search out faulty passages in our lives for condem-
nation and cavalierly neglect the mass of our blessings?
We should then be imitating mean and greedy misers
who make no use of their accumulations but wail in
anguish if they are lost.

If you pity the babe because she departed this life unmarried and childless, again you have the consolation of knowing that you yourself enjoyed a full share of such experiences. It is not fair to set a high value upon these matters for those who lack them and a low for those who have them. She has arrived where there is no distress; there is then no need for us to be distressed. Why should we be afflicted with grief on her account when she herself can experience no grief? The loss of treasures loses its sting when they reach a state to which the sting is no longer appropriate. It was only of little things that your Timoxena was deprived, for all she knew was little things, and in little things she took her pleasure. How can we say that she was deprived of things of which she had no knowledge, no experience, no desire?

You have often heard the assertion made—and the majority find it convincing—that the departed suffer no evil or distress whatever. You will not credit such assertions, I know, because of our ancestral doctrines and the mystic symbols of the Dionysiac initiations with which we have our intimate and shared bond. The soul is incorruptible, and you must imagine that its experience is like that of a caged bird. If it has been maintained in the body for a long time and has become habituated to this life by numerous concerns and long custom, then when it is lifted out it snuggles into the body again, as a bird in its cage, and by repeated births does not forego or cease being involved in the passions and chances of this world. Do not think that old age is vilified and abused because of wrinkles and hoary hair and bodily failure; the most grievous defect of old age is that it renders the soul forgetful of the memories of yonder world and preoccupied with the things of this world, and it is so far bent and distorted that it retains the posture into which it was forced by the body. But the soul which remains in the body but a short span and is then liberated quickly recovers its natural form, for the constraint which was put upon it was but mild and gentle. Fire which has been just quenched can be rekindled by fanning and quickly resumes its strength: and so it is with the soul which has remained but a short while in the body. It is made to pass the gates of death as quickly as possible, before it conceives too great a love for the things of this world and is rendered effeminate by the body and fused with it as by some drug.

The truth concerning these matters is emphasized in our ancient and traditional laws and usages. For those who die in infancy we do not offer the libations or other funeral rites which are customary in the case of other dead because children have no share in earth or earthly concerns. Nor do we visit their tombs and monuments or keep solemn wakes at their bodies. Our laws do not permit such practices because it is an impious thing to mourn for those who are so quickly translated to a better region and a divine lot. And now inasmuch as it is harder to reject our traditions than to trust them, let us comport ourselves outwardly as the laws prescribe, and let our inward conduct be even more untainted and pure and sensible. [*The remainder is wanting.*]

The Education of Children

This is the only complete treatise on education which has come down from antiquity, and it has been the most widely and eagerly studied in the Plutarchan corpus. There are more manuscripts of it than of any other, it exerted enormous influence on the Humanists and their followers, and it continues to be the basis for the opening chapter in histories of education. Paradoxically, the preponderant weight of philological scholarship denies Plutarchan authorship on grounds of certain immaturities in matter and form and certain divergences from normal Plutarchan linguistic usage; on the other hand, a scholar like H. I. Marrou, whose *History of Education in Antiquity* is the best modern treatment of its subject, is willing to accept *The Education of Children* as genuine Plutarch. Whether or not the treatise is from Plutarch's hand it fits admirably into his corpus. Its approach and attitude is quite characteristically Plutarchan, and it does offer a competent precipitate of Platonic, Stoic, and other ancient doctrine on its subject. In its specific prescriptions and in the ethical premises upon which the whole educational process is based, the treatise can still claim the interest of anyone concerned with the problems of education.

WHAT CAN BE SAID regarding the education of freeborn children? What procedures are likely to produce soundness of character? Let us address ourselves to this problem.

Perhaps it is better to begin with parentage as a starting point. Those who desire to become fathers of reputable children I should for my part advise not to consort with any women that happen along, I mean such as courtesans or concubines. Persons not well born, either on their mother's side or their father's, are pursued by the indelible disgrace of bad birth throughout their lives, and any who wish to chide or revile them have an insult ready to hand. Wise indeed was the poet [Euripides] who said

[*Mad Heracles* 1261]: "And if their birth's foundation be not well and truly laid, of necessity children are unfortunate."

Respectable birth therefore affords a man the treasured freedom to speak his mind openly, and the highest value should be set upon it by anyone whose object is lawful procreation. It is perfectly natural for those whose birth is flawed or tainted to be lamed and humbled in their self-esteem, and the poet [Euripides] is quite right in remarking [*Hippolytus* 424], "It makes a slave of a man, however stouthearted he be, when he learns his mother's or father's baseness." By obvious corollary children of distinguished parents are full of proud and lofty temper. Of Cleophantus, for example, the son of Themistocles, it is told that he repeatedly and publicly declared that whatever he wished the commonalty of Athens agreed to: whatever he desired his mother did also; and whatever his mother desired Themistocles did also; and whatever Themistocles desired all the Athenians did also. The Lacedaemonians too merit praise for their lofty temper. They imposed a fine upon their king Archidamus because he persisted in taking to wife a woman of short stature; he intended, said they, to supply them not with monarchs but with monarchins.

Here it is germane to mention a matter which our predecessors, indeed, have not overlooked. And what may it be? It is that husbands who approach their wives for the sake of procreation should properly make their addresses after either total abstinence from wine or only moderate indulgence. When fathers chance to inaugurate the sowing of their seed in inebriation, the children are likely to become winebibbers and topers. That is why Diogenes said, when he observed an unbalanced and maudlin lad, "Young fellow, your father was drunk when he begot you." This must suffice for the subject of birth: I must now treat of education.

To speak in general terms, what we customarily say with reference to the arts and sciences we may say with reference to virtue also: for any wholly correct action three factors must contribute simultaneously, and these are nature, reason, and habit. Reason I define as learning, and habit as practice. The beginnings come from nature, progress from learning, applied use from rehearsing, and the complete whole from all together. In the degree that any of these factors is wanting, in that degree must virtue be lame. Nature without learning is blind, learning apart from nature is fractional, and practice in the absense of both is aimless. Agriculture offers an analogy: in the first place there must be good soil, then the cultivator must be expert, and then the seed must be sound; after the same fashion nature corresponds to the soil, the educator to the cultivator, and the substance of his doctrine and his admonitions to the seed. All of these factors, I would firmly maintain, combined and conspired in the souls of Pythagoras and Socrates and Plato and all who have attained fame eternal.

It is a blessed thing and a mark of divine favor if ever any god has given all these gifts to one man. But if anyone supposes that those who lack natural gifts but are successful in learning and in correct practice of virtue cannot adequately supply their shortcomings in respect to nature, he must be told that he is wide of the mark or rather totally mistaken. As an excellent nature is corrupted by sloth, a sluggish one is uplifted by instruction; easy tasks elude the indifferent, difficult ones are overcome by diligence. How effective and productive diligence and industry can be you may learn by observing many ordinary phenomena. Drops of water hollow out rocks, steel and bronze are rubbed away by the touch of hands, and when toil has imposed its curve on chariot wheels there is no way for them to recover straightness. The crooked staves of actors it is impossible to straighten out, for toil has made the unnatural to prevail over the natural. And are these the only instances which demonstrate the efficacy of diligence? No indeed, there are thousands upon tens of thousands. A piece of land is naturally good, but if it is neglected it runs to waste, and in the degree that it is naturally superior, in the same degree does neglect work greater corruption upon it if it is not worked. Another piece may

be rougher and harder than is proper, but if it is cultivated
it produces sound crops at once. Do not all trees grow
crooked and prove barren if they are disregarded? And yet
if they are trained aright they become fruitful and productive. Do not all faculties of the body fade and wither
because of neglect and rankness and bad conditioning?
But does not even a weak constitution yield marked access
of strength for those who undergo gymnastic training?
Horses too—are they not tractable to their riders if they
have been well broken as colts? And if they remain un-
broken, are they not stiff-necked and willful? But we need
not be astonished at other instances when we see that toil
can make some of the wildest of animals tame and docile.
When the Thessalian was asked who were the most peace-
ful of the Thessalians, he gave an excellent answer:
"Those who are done with fighting." But there is no need
to expatiate. Character is inured habit, and if a man
should call virtues of character virtues of habit, he should
not be marked wrong. In this connection I will make use of
just one more example and then give over expanding on
the subject.

Lycurgus, the lawgiver of the Lacedaemonians, took
two puppies from the same litter and brought them up in
quite different ways, so that one turned out greedy and
thievish, and the other a competent tracker and hunter.
Then when the Lacedaemonians were gathered in assembly, he said, "For acquiring excellence, ye Lacedaemonians, habit and training and instruction and discipline
have very great weight; I shall now make it plain to you
that this is so." He then brought forward the two puppies,
put directly before them a dish and a hare, and unleashed
them. The one darted after the hare, the other rushed to
the dish. The Lacedaemonians could not conjecture why
he had exhibited the puppies and what the demonstration
signified. "Both these dogs," said he, "come from the same
litter, but they have had different upbringing, so that one
has turned out a glutton and the other a hunter." So much
for habits and ways of life.

The subject of feeding is next in order. Mothers, I
would say, should feed their own children and themselves

give them the breast. They will nurture them more sympathetically and with greater care, for they love their children from the depths and, as the expression has it, down to their toenails. But the affection of wet nurses and governesses is spurious and constrained, for they love for hire. Nature itself makes it plain that mothers should themselves nurture and sustain what they have brought forth: for every animal which brings forth nature has provided a supply of milk. Wise indeed is nature's forethought. It has endowed women with two breasts, so that if they bear twins they may have a double source of sustenance. Yet aside from this consideration mothers would come to be more affectionate and loving to their children. It is quite reasonable, by Zeus; comradeship in feeding makes a close bond of affection. Beasts who are separated from their feeding companions give plain indications that they miss them.

As I have said, then, mothers must make every effort to nurse their own children. But if this should prove impossible either because of some physical deficiency (things of this sort do happen) or because they are in haste to bear other children, wet nurses and governesses must not be chosen at random but care must be exercised to obtain the best possible. First of all they must be Greek in character. For just as it is essential that an infant's bodily members be molded immediately from birth so that they may grow straight and undistorted, so is it proper to regulate the character of children from the beginning. Youth is pliant and impressionable, and lessons should be fused into their spirits while they are still soft; things grown hard are not easy to mold. Just as seals leave a sharp impression on soft wax, so are lessons sharply impressed on our souls when we are still children. In my judgment the divine Plato struck the right note when he advised nurses to exercise careful choice even in telling stories to children, so that their minds should not at the outset be filled with foolishness and vice. Phocylides the poet would seem to be offering excellent advice when he says, "While yet a child he should be taught noble actions."

And here is another matter which should not be neglected. When we appoint slave children to be servants and companions to our nurselings, we should seek out first of all such as are mannerly in their conduct and speak precise and lucid Greek, so that our children shall not be contaminated by alien and contemptible characters and take on some of their vulgarity. The familiar adage is quite pertinent: "If you live with a cripple you will learn to limp."

When they reach an age to be put under tutors, special care must be exercised in selecting them; we must not out of negligence turn our children over to slaves or barbarians or undependable persons. As things now are, the practice of people generally is utterly ridiculous. Of their serious-minded slaves, they appoint some to be farm bailiffs, some masters of their shipping, some mercantile agents, some managers, and some bankers: but if they find that a slave is a toper and glutton and useless for any business, they take their sons and surrender them to him. But the tutor ought to be a sound man, with a character like that of Phoenix who was tutor to Achilles.

I now come to the greatest and indeed paramount consideration. The teachers we select for our children must live lives immune to scandal, be irreproachable in conduct, and conversant with respectable society. The fountain and root of gentlemanliness is the acquisition of traditional education. Just as farmers put stakes beside their nurselings so do traditional and responsible teachers fix precepts and admonitions beside their youthful charges so that their characters may sprout straight up. Worthy of the utmost scorn are certain of our present-day fathers who, without making any scrutiny of those who profess to teach, hand their sons over, because of ignorance or sometimes because of inexperience, to reprobates and frauds. If they do so because of inexperience the situation is not so ludicrous; but the height of absurdity is reached—can you suppose when?—when people who know, who have learned from what others have told them, that certain teachers are inexperienced or depraved, nevertheless deliver their children over to them. Some do it because they are overcome by the flatteries of people bent on ingratiating themselves, and there are others who do it out of complaisance to insistent friends. Their procedure furnishes an exemplum—like a man suffering from a bodily infirmity who rejects the expert who could save him and, out of complaisance to a friend, chooses a novice who might kill him; or like a man who dismisses a first-rate skipper and approves of an incompetent at the behest of a friend. Zeus and his holy company! Can a man who calls himself a father take more account of gratifying his petitioners than of the education of his children?

Socrates, the great sage of antiquity, used to say, and very aptly, that if such a thing were possible he would ascend to the loftiest height of the city and cry out: "Where, mankind, are you heading? Upon the acquisition of money you bestow every zeal, but of your sons, to whom you will leave this money, you take little thought." For my part I should add that the procedure of such fathers is very like that of a man who would take thought for his shoe but neglect his foot. But many fathers reach such a pitch in their love of money as well as hatred of children that to avoid paying a larger stipend they choose as teachers for their children men worth nothing at all, shopping for ignorance at bargain prices. On this point Aristippus very neatly and with great cleverness made a jesting remark to a father who had no sense and no brains. When the man asked him his price for educating his son, he replied "A thousand drachmas." "By Heracles," the man said, "what an exorbitant figure! I can buy a slave for a thousand." "Then you will have two slaves," Aristippus retorted, "your son and the fellow you buy." In a word, is it not absurd to accustom a child to receive his food in his right hand and scold him if he puts out his left, and yet to make no provision that he should hear correct and respectable discourse?

What happens to these remarkable fathers when they have brought their sons up and educated them badly? I will tell you. When upon attaining their majority their sons disdain a wholesome and orderly way of life and dive into disorderly and slavish pleasures, the fathers repent having betrayed their children's education and, when regret is futile, they deplore their wrongdoing. Some of the sons take on flatterers and parasites, fellows without character, execrable perverters and corrupters of youth. Others buy the services of mistresses and harlots, creatures insolent and extravagant. Some gourmandize their substance away and others founder upon dice and debauchery. Some even rush into evils more audacious yet, such as adultery and bacchanalian orgies, and incur capital punishment for the sake of a single debauch. But if these men had become habitués of philosophy perhaps they would not have been overborne by such courses. They would at least have learned that injunction of Diogenes, coarsely expressed, to be sure, but factually correct; "Go into any brothel," he says, "and you will learn that what you pay for is no different from what [you can do for yourself and] costs nothing."

In sum I assert (and what I say may be accounted an oracular utterance rather than mere admonition) that the one principal factor in these matters, beginning, middle, and end, is sound upbringing and traditional education, and I declare that it is this which carries a man forward and helps him to achieve excellence and happiness. All other goals are commonplace and petty and not worthy of effort. Good birth is a fine thing, but the merit is our ancestors'. Wealth brings honor, but it is at the disposal of fortune, who frequently takes it away from those who hold it and bestows it upon others who had not hoped for it. Great wealth is the bull's-eye at which those who crave our purses shoot—rascally slaves and blackmailers. Worst of all, even the vilest scoundrels may possess wealth. Reputation is impressive but unstable. Beauty is a prize eagerly sought, but its span is short. Health is an asset but it is subject to mutations. Strength is an enviable quality but an easy victim of disease and age. In general, anyone who prides himself on a robust physique must be informed that his attitude is mistaken. How trivial is any human strength compared with the power of other creatures! Think of elephants and bulls and lions.

Of all our qualities learning alone is immortal and divine. The two factors which are peculiarly characteristic of human nature are intelligence and discourse. Of these intelligence holds dominion over discourse, and discourse is the minister of intelligence. It is impregnable to fortune, immune to calumny, uncorrupted by disease, unimpaired by age. Only intelligence grows young with years, and time which diminishes all things else increases understanding for the aging. War sweeps all things away like a torrent and carries them off; learning alone war has no power to ravage. Memorable indeed, in my judgment, is the utterance of the Megarian philosopher, Stilpo. When Demetrius had enslaved the people of that city and leveled it to the ground, he asked Stilpo whether he had incurred any loss. "None at all," rejoined Stilpo, "war cannot plunder virtue." Of the same pitch and measure, it seems, was the response of Socrates. When Gorgias, I believe it was, asked him his opinion of the king of Persia and whether he considered him a happy man, Socrates replied, "I do not know how he stands with respect to virtue and learning." Evidently he judged that happiness is comprised in these factors and not in the benefits of fortune.

As earnestly as I advise that the education of children must be made the chiefest of all cares, so also do I urge cleaving to the uncorrupted and wholesome kind of education: the young must be kept at the furthest remove from the silly display of carnival orators. To please the mob is to displease the wise. What I say is corroborated by the lines of Euripides [*Hippolytus* 986]: "I have no skill in speaking before the crowd; I am cleverer, on the other hand, with my friends, and those few. That too is quite natural; those who are accounted of no consequence among the wise are eloquent before the mob." My own observation is that those who take pains to make their speech pleasing and ingratiating to the vulgar rabble also generally lead intemperate and voluptuous lives. And necessarily so, by Zeus. If in providing pleasures for other men they give no heed to what is honorable, then surely they would be unlikely to rate uprightness and wholesomeness above self-gratification and indulgence or to pursue prudence rather than pleasure.

Furthermore, why should children . . . [*lacuna*]? Neither

to speak nor to act at random is a good thing, and, as the proverb says, good things are hard. Extemporaneous speeches are deft and facile to abundance, but those who make them know neither where to begin nor where to stop. Aside from their other mistakes, people who speak on the spur of the moment fall into frightful and endless garrulity. It is reflection which prevents a speech from overflowing appropriate bounds. Pericles, "as hath been recounted for our edification," when the people invited him to speak, frequently refused on the grounds that he was unprepared. And Demosthenes too, who zealously emulated Pericles' policy, resisted the Athenians who solicited his counsel, declaring "I am not prepared." This tradition may be fictional and without authority, but in his speech against Midias he sets forth the usefulness of reflection very clearly. Here are his words: "I declare, men of Athens, that I have reflected on this matter, and would not deny that I have rehearsed it as carefully as I could. Feckless indeed should I be if, considering the treatment I have received and am receiving, I had taken no thought of what I should say to you about it." Yet I should by no means insist that readiness of speech should always be despised; it should be used on appropriate occasions, but should be applied like a drug. Until a man has reached maturity I hold that he should never speak extemporaneously; but when his powers have taken firm root, then if the opportune occasion suggests such a course he may properly exercise freedom in his discourse. People who have been fettered for a long while are unable, by reason of long habituation to bonds, to stride freely, but even when they are liberated walk circumspectly. It is the same with people who have long throttled their speech: even if they should be required to speak without premeditation their exposition nevertheless preserves its wonted character. But license for the immature to speak extemporaneously is the proven source of vain babbling. They say that a wretched painter remarked to Apelles, as he showed him a picture, "This I have just now painted." "Even without your telling me," said Apelles, "I know that it was painted hastily. I wonder that you have not painted more like it."

To return to the main subject of my discourse, my advice is that just as a speaker should beware of a theatrical and melodramatic style, so too should he avoid the petty and commonplace. Turgidity is unstatesmanlike, meagerness too unimpressive. Just as the body should be not only sound but also healthy, so speech should be not only free from sickness but also sturdy. Safety is only commended, boldness admired. My opinion in regard to the psychological attitude of a speaker is, as it happens, the same. He should be neither audacious nor spiritless and cowering, for the one attitude settles into impudence, the other into servility. To cleave to the middle course in all things is the mark of the expert and painstaking craftsman.

While I am still dealing with training and offering my opinion on the subject, I should like to say that in the first place I consider a discourse composed of simple sentences palpable evidence of inadequate education. Secondly, I believe that such a practice cloys and always begets impatience, whereas variety is delightful; this is the case in every performance directed to sight or hearing.

Nor ought we permit the freeborn child to miss performances directed to sight and hearing any more than other subjects in what is called general education. But these he should learn by the way, merely to sample them, as it were, for perfection in all things is unattainable; but the prime place belongs to philosophy. I can illustrate my meaning by an example. To travel about and visit many cities is a fine thing, but it is profitable to settle down in the best. The philosopher Bion put the case very wittily: just as the suitors, when they could get no access to Penelope, consorted with her maidservants, so those who are incapable of attaining philosophy wear themselves to the bone over trivial subjects. Hence it follows that philosophy must be made the prime object of education. For the care of the body men have discovered two sciences, medicine and gymnastics, of which the one bestows health and the other robustness. But for the diseases and distempers of the mind philosophy is the sole remedy. Through philosophy, and with it, a man may understand what is noble and what is base, what is just and what unjust, what, in a word, is to be chosen and what is to be avoided; how he should demean himself to the gods, to his parents, to his elders, to the laws, to strangers, to magistrates, to friends, to women, to children, to servants; that he should revere the gods, honor his parents, respect his elders, obey the laws, defer to the magistrates, love his friends, be chaste towards women, affectionate towards children, not lord it over servants; and most important, not to be overjoyed in prosperity nor overdejected in adversity, not to be dissolute in pleasures nor uncontrolled and brutish in anger.

Of all the advantages that accrue from philosophy these I reckon the chiefest. To bear prosperity like a gentleman is the mark of a man, to deprecate envy the mark of a disciplined character, to rise superior to pleasure by reason the mark of a sage, to govern anger the mark of an extraordinary man. But as perfect men I regard those who are able to mingle and fuse political capacity with philosophy. Such men, I take it, are masters of the two greatest goods there are: as statesmen, a life of public usefulness, and a tranquil existence of untroubled serenity in the pursuit of philosophy. Among the three possible types of life—the practical, the contemplative, and the pleasure-seeking— the last is dissolute and enslaved to pleasure, and hence bestial and undignified; the contemplative, wanting practical application, is useless; and the practical, having no share in philosophy, is uncultured and common. We must apply our best endeavors, therefore, both to perform public duties and to hold fast to philosophy as far as opportunity permits. So did Pericles shape his career, so did Archytas of Tarentum (who became a companion of Plato), so did Epaminondas of Thebes.

On the subject of training, then, I do not know why I need take time to say more. But to supplement what has been said, it is useful, or rather essential, not to be negligent about acquiring the writings of the ancients. One ought to make a collection of these as a farmer collects tools. The use of books is to education what a tool is to a farmer; by such use we are enabled to study knowledge from its source.

Well then, exercise of the body must also not be overlooked, but boys should be sent to the trainer's to attain competence in such matters also, for the sake both of graceful bearing and a sturdy body. A sound constitution in boyhood is the foundation for a vigorous old age; and just as fair weather is the time to make preparations against a storm, so in youth we should store up orderliness and temperance as a viaticum for old age. But physical labor should be dispensed economically; boys should not be so exhausted as to be incapable of the effort required for study. Sleep and weariness, according to Plato, are the enemies of learning. What is the point of these remarks? I hasten to mention the most important factor in this context. It is in warlike exercises that boys must be practiced; they must train in javelin throwing, in archery, and in hunting. In battle [as Xenophon says], "the goods of the vanquished stand as prizes for the victors." War does not tolerate a shade-grown physique; a sinewy soldier inured to warlike exercise thrusts aside phalanxes of puffed-out athletes.

"What is this?" someone may say, "you promised, did you not, to give precepts for the education of freeborn children? But now it develops that you disregard the education of the poor citizenry and are openly limiting your suggestions to the rich." To such objections it is not difficult to reply. My own dearest wish is that my curriculum should be advantageous to all alike; but if some, by reason of their own needy state, are unable to avail themselves of my precepts, they must find fault with fortune, not with the promulgator of the precepts. And yet even the poor must endeavor to provide the best possible education for their children; if they cannot provide the best, they must use what resources they can. These extra observations I have inserted into my discourse so that I might effect an orderly transition to the remaining themes relevant to the proper education of the young.

And here is my next point. I assert that children should be induced to gentlemanly behavior by admonition and reasoning, not, in heaven's name, by blows and torments. It must be obvious that such treatment is appropriate rather to slaves than to freemen. They grow lethargic and recoil from their tasks, partly because of the pain of the blows, partly because of the degradation. For the freeborn, praise and blame are more effective than any abuse whatever; praise incites them to excellence, blame deters them from shamefulness.

But reproof and commendation must be employed alternately and variously: whenever they grow bold, they should be reduced to modesty by reproof, and then again be encouraged by commendation; we should imitate the practice of nurses who, when they have made their babies cry, again offer the breast to comfort them. But neither must we exalt and puff them up with encomia; excess of praise inflates conceit and enervates.

I have even seen fathers in whom excessive love became the cause of absence of love. I shall illustrate with an example, to clarify my meaning. In their eagerness for their children to take first place in everything quickly, they impose disproportionate tasks upon them. These the children cannot perform and so fail; moreover, they are depressed by their unhappy experience and so do not receive instruction with docility. Just as plants are nourished by modest applications of water but are choked by excess, so the mind grows by proportionate assignments but is submerged by a plethora. We must therefore give children respite from unremitting toil, bearing in mind that all human life is divided between intensity and relaxation. In keeping with this division we have not only wakefulness but also sleep, not only war but also peace, not only tempests but also calm, not only working periods but also festivals. To put the matter briefly, rest is the sauce of labor. We may observe that this principle applies not only to living creatures but also to inanimate objects: bows and lyres we unstring, in order that we may be able to tense them again. To generalize, the body is kept in condition by emptying and filling, the mind by relaxation and toil.

Such fathers as commit their sons to tutors and teachers and themselves never at all witness or overhear their instructions deserve rebuke, for they fall far short of their obligation. They ought themselves to undertake examination of their children every few days and not place their trust in the disposition of a wage earner; even the latter will bestow greater care on the children if they know that they will periodically be called to account. Here the witty saying of the hostler is apt: nothing fattens the horse so much as the king's eye.

It is most important to train and habituate the children's memory. Memory is, as it were, the larder of learning. That is why myth represents Mnemosyne [Memory] as the mother of the Muses, plainly intimating thereby that nothing is so fit to beget and nurture learning as memory. For either alternative, therefore, memory must be exercised, whether children are naturally endowed with retentive memory or whether they are forgetful. The bounty of nature one must strengthen, her deficiency we must supply, and so boys with good memories will surpass others, those with bad will surpass themselves. Excellent is Hesiod's saying: "If to little you add but little, so you do this steadily, soon will it be big." This too fathers must realize, that the memorizing aspect of learning contributes no small share not only to education but also to the practical conduct of life, for the memory of past deeds provides examples in taking good counsel for the future.

This too: we must keep our sons from nasty speech, for, according to Democritus, "the word is the shadow of the deed." Furthermore provision must be made that they be courteous and affable in their address. No trait so earns dislike as tactlessness, and boys can avoid becoming odious to their fellows by not proving wholly intransigent in discussions. To understand not only how to win but also how to lose is an advantage where winning is harmful; there is indeed such a thing as a Cadmean victory. For this I can cite the testimony of sage Euripides, who says: "When two converse and one's passion rises, he that yields in argument is wiser."

Now I must mention certain rules of conduct which the young should cultivate not less but more carefully than those already dealt with, to wit: To practice the simple life, to restrain the tongue, to rise above anger, to govern one's hands. We must examine the substance of each of these rules; examples will make them more intelligible.

I shall begin with the last. Some men by stretching their

hands out to unjust profit have squandered the reputation
their earlier course had gained. Gylippus the Lacedaemonian is an example: he unstitched the money bags, and
so was exiled from Sparta.

Control of anger, furthermore, is the mark of a wise
man. Socrates was once kicked by an obstreperous and
odious stripling, whereupon those in his company were out-
raged and in their indignation were intent on requiting him.
"What," said Socrates, "if an ass had kicked me? Would
you think it right to kick him back?" Nor did that young
fellow get off with impunity; when everyone reviled him
and nicknamed him Kicker he hanged himself.

Socrates was showered with every possible sort of abuse
in Aristophanes' *Clouds*. When the play was presented a
man who attended it said to Socrates, "Are you not indignant at being made such a butt?" "Not I, by Zeus,"
said Socrates, "I take banter in the theater as if it were a
big private party." Archytas of Tarentum and Plato behaved in a kindred and parallel manner, as we shall soon
see. Archytas returned from the wars, where he had been
general, and found his land run to ruin. He summoned his
bailiff and said, "You'd have something to wail about if
I were not too angry." Plato was incensed at a greedy and
rascally slave; he called his sister's son Speusippus and went
off, saying, "Beat this fellow, I am too incensed." But such
conduct is difficult, it may be objected, and hard to imitate.
I am perfectly aware that it is. But we must endeavor, as
far as in us lies, to follow these models and rid ourselves of
a large part of our ungoverned and furious anger. In other
respects too we cannot rival those models, neither in experience nor in nobility. But no less than they are we, as
it were, mystagogues and torchbearers of wisdom, and we
must seek, so far as in us lies, to emulate and sample these
patterns.

There remains, of the topics I proposed to discuss, that
of the governance of the tongue. If anyone supposes that
this is a trivial or common matter he is far astray from the
truth. A sage thing is timely silence, and better than any
speech. It is for this reason, I do believe, that the ancients
instituted the procedures for initiation into the mysteries,

so that, having grown accustomed to maintain silence in the mysteries, we may transfer the reverence appropriate to divine secrets to fidelity in keeping human mysteries. No one has ever regretted having kept silence, but very many have regretted chattering. It is easy to utter what has been kept silent, but impossible to recall what has been uttered. I know countless instances of men who have fallen into the gravest calamities through their tongue's intemperance. I shall mention one or two as typical, and omit the rest. When Ptolemy Philadelphus married his sister Arsinoe, Sotades said, "The thrust of that goad is misdirected," and rotted in prison for many years. For his unseasonable babbling he paid a penalty none could find unmerited, and to provide laughter for others he purchased long sorrow for himself. A mate to this story and a rival to it, but much more dreadful, is what the sophist Theocritus said and suffered. Alexander had ordered the Greeks to prepare crimson robes in order to celebrate sacrifices for his victory in the war against the barbarians, and the states assessed so much per head. "I was always in doubt," said Theocritus, "what Homer meant by 'crimson death'; now I understand perfectly." This got him Alexander for an enemy. Antigonus, the Macedonian king, who was one-eyed, Theocritus provoked to extreme anger by reproaching him with his defect. Antigonus had sent his chef Eutropion, who had served in his army, to summon Theocritus, for he wished to exchange views with him. When Eutropion delivered his message and repeatedly insisted upon it, Theocritus said, "I know that you wish to serve me up raw to that Cyclops"—chiding the one for being disfigured and the other for being a cook. "Then you shall lose your head," said Eutropion. "You shall pay the price for your wide-open mouth and your folly." He reported the conversation to the king, who sent and put Theocritus to death.

Besides all this we have an obligation, and a most sacred one, to accustom children to speak the truth. Lying is a slavish habit, despicable in the eyes of all, and even in decent slaves it is not to be condoned.

What I have said above with reference to the decent and temperate behavior of boys I have said without hesitation or qualification. But in regard to what is next to be dealt with my mind is divided and I am of two opinions. I am inclined this way and that, like scales in balance, and am unable to settle down on either side. I am loath to introduce the subject, loath too to turn away from it; but nevertheless I must find courage to speak out. The question is this: whether we should permit the suitors of our boys to associate with them and pass their time with them, or whether the opposite policy of excluding them and shooing them away from intimacy with our boys is correct. Whenever I look at blunt-spoken fathers of the austere and astringent type who regard intimacy with lovers an intolerable outrage upon their sons, I am circumspect about showing myself a sponsor and advocate of the practice. But on the other hand, when I reflect upon Socrates, Plato, Xenophon, Aeschines, Cebes and that whole troop of men who gave their approval to male loves and guided adolescents towards culture and political leadership and excellence of character, I am again of another mind and am swayed by emulation of those worthies. Euripides gives testimony in their favor in his lines: "Another love subsists among human kind, the love of a just and temperate and noble soul." Nor can Plato's saying, in which earnest and banter are mingled, be overlooked. He declares that men who have proven their worth should be permitted to caress any fair lad they please. Lovers who lust only for physical beauty, then, it is right to drive away; but free access should be granted to the lovers of the soul. Such loves as those in Thebes and Elis and the so-called "rapes" in Crete are to be avoided; those in Athens and in Lacedaemon are to be emulated.

In regard to these matters, then, each man may take a position in accordance with his own convictions. As for myself, now that I have spoken concerning the orderly and decorous deportment of children I shall move on to the period of adolescence and make some brief remarks on the subject. I have frequently found fault with those who are in effect sponsors of wicked habits: their boys they put in charge of tutors and teachers, but when the boys reach adolescence they allow their impulses to range unfettered. This is a perversity; greater caution and vigilance are requisite for adolescents than for boys. Everyone knows that the derelictions of boys are trivial and easy to mend—slighting their tutors, perhaps, or misleading their teachers and failure to attend to their lessons. But when they have reached adolescence their offenses are often monstrously wicked—gourmandizing, pilfering money from their parents, dicing, reveling, drinking, love affairs with girls, and corruption of married women. It follows that their impulses must be restrained and fettered by careful supervision. The ripeness of adolescence is prodigal in pleasures, skittish, and in need of a bridle; if parents do not grasp hold of this period with a firm hand, their folly gives license to iniquity. It is therefore incumbent upon sensible fathers to watch over this particular period with special vigilance and to keep their adolescents temperate by instruction, by threats, by entreaties, by pointing out examples of men whom love of pleasure has thrown into misfortune and of those whose perseverance has won them commendation and high repute. These two factors—hope of distinction and fear of punishment—are, as it were, the elements of excellence; the one spurs men on to eagerness for the noblest of pursuits, while the other renders them loath to follow ignoble practices.

In general it is proper to keep the young from association with wicked people, for they carry away some part of their baseness. This principle Pythagoras has enjoined in enigmatical rules, which I shall now put before you and expound. Their contribution adds no small weight to the impulse towards acquiring excellence. For example:

"Do not taste black-tail fish," that is, do not pass your time with men whose character is black with vice.

"Do not step over the beam of a balance," that is, justice should be very highly esteemed and must not be transgressed.

"Do not sit upon a peck measure,"—or eschew sloth, and take thought how we may provide ourselves with necessities.

"Do not put out your hand to everyone"—stands for "One must not strike up friendships too readily."

"Do not wear a tight ring," which means that one ought to keep his life free and not subject it to any fetter.

"Do not stir fire with steel" stands for "Do not provoke a man in a passion." Indeed one shouldn't, but rather yield to men who are angry.

"Do not eat your heart"—or, do not afflict your soul by consuming it with anxieties.

"Abstain from beans," which means that one should not engage in politics; in the olden times beans served as ballots for impeaching magistrates.

"Do not put food in a chamber pot." This signifies that it is not seemly to put clever speech into a foul mind; for speech is the food of thought, and the foulness in men makes it unclean.

"Do not turn back on approaching the goal"—that is, when men are about to die and see the goal of life at hand, they should bear it with equanimity and not be dispirited.

But I return to the original proposition of this discourse: as I said, the young should be kept away from all wicked men, and particularly from flatterers. What I have continually and repeatedly said to many fathers I should like to say here: There is no class more pernicious, none that unhinges youth more quickly and surely than that of flatterers. Both father and son they ruin root and branch, filling the old age of the one and the youth of the other with sorrow, rendering the hook of their evil counsel irresistible by covering it with a bait of pleasure. Sons of wealthy families their fathers admonish to sobriety, flatterers to drunkenness; fathers to temperance, flatterers to wantonness; fathers to frugality, flatterers to extravagance; fathers to industry, flatterers to sloth. "All life is but a moment," they say, "one should live, not vegetate. Why must we worry about your father's threats? He is a doting fool, a walking corpse; very soon we'll hoist him up and carry him to the graveyard." A flatterer will be his pander and send him a strumpet or procure him a married woman; he ravishes and hews down what fathers have provided for old age. Cursed is their tribe! They put on the mask of friendship, and have never tasted frank speech; they toady to the rich and despise the poor. They are virtuosi in seducing the young. When their livelihood is amused, they bare their teeth in a grin; they are supposititious specimens of spirit, bastard portions of humanity. They live at the beck and nod of the rich; chance has made them freeborn, their own choice slaves. It is when they are not treated with insult that they feel insulted, because then their free board is pointless. And so if any father is concerned for the proper upbringing of his children, he must drive these abominable creatures away. And it is no less important that he drive vicious schoolmates away, for these too are capable of corrupting even the best constituted characters.

The foregoing observations present what is excellent and advantageous; what I now propose to say relates to human nature. To resume with the fathers: in my judgment they should not be harsh and unbending in nature but concede certain slips to their juniors, remembering that they were themselves once young. Just as physicians, by mixing bitter medicines with sweet syrups, have found the agreeable a vehicle for the wholesome, so should fathers mingle the sharpness of their fault-finding with gentleness. Sometimes they should slacken the reins and give play to their children's desires, and then again draw them taut. Most important, they should bear their errors without passion; if they do not, and on occasion flare into a rage, the flame should burn down quickly. It is better for a father's temper to be quick than to be heavy; sullennness and implacability is no small indication that he hates his children. It is a good thing too to pretend not to notice certain of their slips, but to turn an old man's dim eye and dull ear to what goes on; in the case of certain behavior it is good having eyes to see not, ears to hear not. Our friends' shortcomings we tolerate: is it remarkable that we should do the same for our children? Though slaves show the effects of a hangover, we do not tax them with their spree. You were stingy once; be openhanded as well. You were angry once; be forgiving as well. Once he tricked you through a slave; check your anger. Once he took a yoke of cattle from the field, once he came home with yesterday's potting on his breath;

take no notice of it. And if the reek is of a woman's perfumery, hold your peace. This is the way a skittish colt is
broken in.

In the case of those who are weaker than their desires
and inaccessible to reproof, an effort should be made to
harness them with the yoke of matrimony, which is the
surest hobble for youth. But the wives we betroth to our
sons should not be too much their superior in birth or
wealth. "Drive in your own corner" is a wise saying. Those
who marry far above their station unwittingly become not
husbands of their wives but slaves of their dowry.

I will add a few remarks more and so bring my precepts
to a close. Above all, by committing no error themselves,
by discharging their full duty, fathers should make themselves shining examples to their children, who may then
look to their fathers' lives as to a mirror and so be deterred
from shameful words and deeds. Those who blame their
errant sons and themselves fall into the same errors are unwittingly prosecuting themselves in the name of their children. If the lives they lead are wholly bad they forfeit the
right to reprove even their slaves freely, let alone their sons.
Furthermore they are likely to prove advocates and teachers
of iniquity to their sons. Where the old men are shameless,
the young must lack all respect.

We must therefore endeavor to follow every practice
which may conduce to the temperance of our children.
Here we emulate the example of Eurydice, who, though she
was an Illyrian and so thrice a barbarian, nevertheless late
in life applied herself to culture for the sake of her children's education. Her devotion to her children is suffi-
ciently indicated by the epigram which she dedicated to
the Muses:

> This monument Eurydice of Hierapolis dedicates to the
> Muses for having attained her soul's desire for knowledge.
> Happy mother of grown sons she labored to learn letters, the
> wardens of wisdom.

The fulfillment of all the precepts presented above is
an ideal for admonition or prayer. Diligent observance of
even the greater part requires good gifts and intense application, but this goal human nature is capable of achieving.

Flattery and Friendship

The full title of this treatise is "How One May Distinguish between Flatterer and Friend." In the opening paragraphs Plutarch makes it clear that the flatterer in question is not the vulgar parasite of New Comedy, who is very easy to recognize, but an associate of some social standing to whose flattery men of position are peculiarly vulnerable because they start by being their own flatterers. The treatise follows a transparent outline, setting forth, through the twenty-fourth Paragraph, the various criteria for distinguishing between the genuine friend and his plausible imitation. The remaining third deals with frank outspokenness *(parrhesia)* which true friends are obligated to apply as therapy and which false friends, because it is a characteristic element in friendship, distort and divert to their own uses. The treatise closes with prescriptions for the judicious and seasonable use of outspokenness.

Character analysis was a special preoccupation of the Peripatetic School. In the *Nicomachean Ethics* (1108a, 1159b) Aristotle had suggested comparisons between friend and flatterer, and his successor Theophrastus had written analyses of friendship. The writing of "comparisons"*(synkriseis)* was a regular feature of the rhetorician's curriculum, and Plutarch frequently employs the device, most notably in the conclusions to his pairs of parallel Lives. Like Plutarch's other treatises, *Flattery and Friendship* affords an insight into ancient social relationships and wholesome edification of perennial relevance.

I F A MAN acknowledges that he cherishes a deep affection for himself, my dear Antiochus Philopappus, everyone is indulgent to him, says Plato [*Laws* 731 de], but Plato also says that such self-love entails many evils, of which the greatest is that it prevents a man from being an honest and unprejudiced judge of himself. "Love is blind as concerns its object," he says, unless a man schools himself to respect and pursue excellence rather than habit and familiarity. This blindness gives the flatterer a wide range, under the heading of love, for he can use our self-love to support his attack; every man is his own prime and greatest flatterer and hence gives ready access to an outsider who corroborates and endorses the high opinion he has framed of himself. The man stigmatized as a lover of flatterers is in fact a lover of himself, and this affection makes him fancy that he possesses every desirable quality. Desire of these qualities is quite normal, but the conviction that one possesses them is dangerous and must be guarded against.

If truth is divine and, as Plato [*Laws* 730 c] puts it, the first principle "of all good for gods, of all good for men," then the chances are that the flatterer is an enemy to the gods, and especially to Apollo. By implanting in a man deception concerning himself and ignorance of himself and of what is good and evil in him he goes counter to the principle of "know thyself." He prevents the good from being perfected and consummated and the evil from being corrected.

If, like other undesirables, the flatterer attached himself only or mainly to the ill-bred and vile, he would not be so formidable or hard to combat. But just as soft and aromatic wood is most susceptible to worms, so aspiring and honorable and decent characters receive and are hosts to the parasite flatterer. "Horse-breeding," Simonides says, "befits not Zacynthus but grain-bearing plains"; similarly we see that flattery attends not upon the needy or obscure or inconsiderable, but makes itself the stumbling-block and plague of large houses and large affairs and frequently subverts kingdoms and principalities. It is no trifling matter, then, nor one requiring but slight application, to analyze flattery and expose its nature as fully as may be, so that it may not taint or cheapen true friendship. Lice leave the dying, they desert bodies in which the blood on which they fed is quenched; and neither are flatterers to be seen infesting fortunes that are sere and chill. They beset distinction and power and wax fat, and they trickle away when fortune veers. But we must not wait for the test of experience; it is needless or even hurtful, with an element of danger. In a crisis which calls for friends it is disastrous to discover that "friends" are false, when it is not possible to exchange the unreliable and spurious for the steadfast and true. Like a coin a friend must be proven genuine before the critical moment, not demonstrated as a counterfeit by the crisis itself. We ought not wait for an injury to open our eyes, but rather to avoid injury by learning how to recognize the flatterer and his works. Otherwise we shall fare as do those who recognize a lethal drug only by taste, and find its potency at the cost of their utter ruin.

We cannot approve of these men, but neither can we approve of those who conceive of a friend as austerely noble and helpful and regard persons whose conversation is affable as flatterers caught red-handed. A friend is not something disagreeable and unseasoned, nor is it puritanical astringency which gives friendship its dignity; nay, its dignity and nobility are comprised in its being sweet and endearing—"By its side the Graces and Yearning have established their dwelling." Not only for the afflicted "It is sweet to gaze into friendly eyes," as Euripides [*Ion* 732] says; and not only does it remove the stings of adversity and heal our helplessness, but it brings satisfaction and delight to our prosperity as well. Fire, Evenus has said, is the most effective sauce; so god has made everything bright and sweet and amiable by seasoning life with friendship and making it a companion in enjoyment. If the flatterer saw that friendship never admitted the agreeable, how could you explain his use of pleasure to insinuate himself? But the flatterer apes the agreeable affability of a friend, just as false and deceptive gilt imitates only the lustrous sheen of gold; he always shows himself gay and charming, never uncomplaisant or disapproving. But it does not follow that we must straightway suspect those who praise us of being flatterers. Seasonable praise is no less appropriate to friendship than blame. Consistent snappishness and faultfinding is unfriendly and unsociable, but we shall accept reproof and outspoken criticism patiently and without offense from a kindly temperament which can also give unstinted and ungrudging praise, because we are confident that a man who is willing to praise blames only where he must for our own good.

If neither pleasure nor praise is a gauge—indeed we observe that flattery frequently outstrips friendship in rendering helpful service—a man might say that it is difficult to distinguish flatterer from friend. It is indeed difficult, we shall agree, if our object is the genuine flatterer who plies his trade with subtle art. There is no difficulty in the case of flatterers in the vulgar sense of the word—those cruet-carrying lick-platters who, as the saying goes, make themselves heard as soon as hands are washed for dinner; their servile character is evident from their vulgarity and buffoonery at the first dish and goblet. It needed no probing, surely, to discover that Melanthius, Alexander of Pherae's parasite, was a flatterer. When people asked him how Alexander was murdered, he said, "By a thrust through his ribs into my belly." Nor can we be in doubt about the swarm around a rich man's table whom "neither fire nor steel nor bronze can keep from a dinner," nor yet about the she-flatterers of Cyprus who were called "she-steps" when they crossed to Syria because they bent over to make backs for the royal ladies to climb into their carriages on.

Who is the man we must watch out for? The man who dissembles and will not acknowledge that he is a flatterer, whom you do not find haunting the kitchen or watching the clock for dinnertime or drop drunk in his tracks; he is usually sober and officious and thinks he must have a hand in everything and wants to share every secret. In short, he plays the role of friend not in the comic or satyric but in the tragic style. Plato says [*Republic* 361 a] the extreme of dishonesty is to seem honest when you are not; so the flattery hardest to cope with is the sort which is covert and not avowed, not the sportive but the sober kind. This sort infects even genuine friendship with mistrust, unless we are alert, for its aspect is often identical. Gobryas dashed after the Magus into a dark room and grappled with him, and Darius hesitated to strike; whereupon Gobryas bade him thrust though he pierce both [*Herodotus* 3.78]. We, of course, can never approve the saying "Perish friend so the foe perish," but must endeavor to separate the flatterer from the friend whom he resembles so closely in so many respects and use the utmost care not to cast the good out with the bad or submit to injury out of solicitude for our own. Imagine separating seeds: if wild seeds of the same shape and size as wheat get mixed up with wheat, it is difficult to winnow them out; if the holes in the sieve are small they cannot pass through, and if large the wheat passes through along with the wild seeds. So is flattery hard to separate from friendship, because it assimilates itself to every mood and movement, every interest and inclination.

But because nothing is so sweet as friendship and nothing gives greater satisfaction, the flatterer makes pleasure his business and uses it as a bait. And because agreeableness and usefulness are concomitants of friendship (which is why we say that a friend is more essential than fire and water), the flatterer obtrudes his services upon us and strives to show himself zealous and indefatigable and devoted. The flatterer observes that what brings people together in the first place and cements their friendship is similarity of pursuits and tastes and identical reactions of attraction or aversion to the same things, and accordingly he adapts and molds himself, like some amorphous mass, in an effort to assimilate himself to his intended victim by process of imitation. So deft are his transformations and so plausible his assimilation that one would say, "Not Achilles' son but himself art thou."

But the greatest roguery of all is this. Observing that outspokenness is said and seems to be the characteristic language of friendship, just as every animal has his characteristic call, and that reserve is boorish and unfriendly, he extends his imitation to cover this too. Just as expert chefs use tart sauces and pungent condiments to counteract the cloying effect of sweet dishes, so flatterers introduce an outspokenness which is neither sincere or helpful but only titillates and grins as it frowns. That is why the man is so hard to detect, like animals whose nature is to camouflage themselves in the color and shape of their environment. Since the flatterer swathes himself in similarity to deceive us, it is our task to unswathe him to show his dissimilarity and reveal him, as Plato [*Phaedrus* 239 d] puts it, "bedizening himself with another's colors and forms for want of his own."

We must proceed with our examination from the beginning. We have stated that in most cases the inception of friendship is a conformity of taste and character and naturally congenial dispositions which find pleasure in the same pursuits and activities and pastimes. As the playwright says:

> Greybeard finds greybeard's tongue sweetest,
> Child child's, and woman consorts with woman;
> Invalid suits invalid, and a man woebegone
> Is charmed by a fellow-sufferer.

The flatterer knows that it is natural for men with similar tastes to conceive affection and intimacy with one another, and accordingly tries to be near his victim and bivouac at his side, as if he were hunting game in a pasture, and calms his skittishness by accommodating himself to his pursuits and pastimes and interests and habits until he takes on his victim's coloring and grasps an opportunity to lay hold of him and tame and habituate him to his touch. He finds fault with whatever actions or careers or persons he notices his victim disapproves of, and praises whatever pleases his victim, not moderately but with astonishment and admiration to surpass his victim's, maintaining all the while that his preferences and aversions are based on judgment, not caprice.

How can we convict the man? What distinguishing marks will prove that he is not and will not become congenial but is only imitating congeniality? First we must look to the consistency and continuance of his preferences to see whether he regularly approves and commends the same things and guides and directs his own life by a single pattern, as becomes a disinterested lover of congeniality and intimacy. That is what a friend is. But the flatterer, because he has no abiding hearth for his character and lives a life not he but another has chosen, because he molds and accommodates his life to another's, is not uniform and consistent but variable and many-colored; like water poured from one container to another, he always assumes the configuration of the receptacle.

You catch a monkey, it seems, when he tries to imitate a man in his swaying and prancing, but the flatterer himself leads others on and entices them by his imitation, varying his technique with the victim, dancing and singing with one, wrestling and rolling in the dust with another. When his quarry is a hunting type he follows all but shouting Phaedra's lines [Euripides, *Hippolytus* 218]: "Gods! I yearn to urge on the dogs, to track the dappled deer!" It is not the game that concerns him: it is the huntsman himself he is trying to trap. If a bookish and studious young man is his quarry, he surrounds himself with books and lets his beard grow down to his feet; now he parades the philosopher's gabardine and indifference, and his talk is all of numbers and Platonic right-angle triangles. Now if some rich and idle toper falls in his way, then "casting his beggarly rags aside deep-plotting Odysseus" [*Odyssey* 22.1] flings off the philosopher's gabardine and shears the beard away like a fruitless crop. Now it's tuns and goblets and guffawing promenades and ridicule of the philosophizers. When Plato arrived in Syracuse, people say, and Dionysius went mad for philosophy, the palace was turned into a sandbox with hordes of geometricians drawing figures in it. When Plato came to grief and Dionysius shook philosophy off to dash back to wine and women and folly and debauchery, everyone was at once seized by philistinism and oblivion and folly as though Circe had bewitched them. Further evidence is supplied by the careers of master flatterers and demagogues, of whom the greatest was Alcibiades. At Athens he was a wit and a *bon vivant* and kept race horses; in Sparta he was close-cropped, wore a gabardine, and bathed in cold water; in Thrace he was a brawler and a drunk; but when he came to Tissaphernes he was effeminate and voluptuous and arrogant. It was by assimilating and accommodating himself to everyone that he won them over and was able to influence them. Very different were Epaminondas and Agesilaus. Though they had contacts with very many individuals and cities and ways of life, they everywhere maintained their own character in dress and habits and speech and way of life. Similarly Plato was the same in Syracuse as he was in the Academy, and the same to Dionysius as to Dion.

Because the flatterer is as changeable as a cuttlefish he can be caught out if his victim too pretends to be changeable, finding fault with a life he previously admired and suddenly approving of actions and behavior and speech which formerly irritated him. Then he will see that the flatterer is at no point consistent or individual, that he does not love or hate, rejoice or grieve, by native reaction, but like a mirror takes on reflections of outsiders' reactions and characters and movements. So characterless a man will say, if he hears you find fault with some friend, "You've found the fellow out at last; I never did like him," and then if you change over and praise the man he will declare, by Zeus, that he shares your satisfaction, that he thanks you on the man's behalf, that he has confidence in him. If you say you must alter your mode of life and change, let us say, from a political career to a life of inactivity and repose, "Relief from tumult and envy," he will declare, "should have come long ago." And then if you contemplate embarking on politics and public speaking again, he will second you and say: "Just what one would expect of you. Idleness is sweet, but it is undistinguished and lowly." To such a man we ought to say directly [*Odyssey* 16.181]: "Wholly another a moment agone, stranger, thou seemedst. A man who follows my every movement and gesture is not the friend I need—my shadow does it better—but one who is sincere in his judgments." This, then, is one criterion for detecting the flatterer.

There is another which we must watch out for—the mode of his imitation. A true friend does not imitate or readily praise everything, but only what is excellent: "Not hatred does he share, but love," as Sophocles [*Antigone* 523] puts it. And he shares right dealing too, by Zeus, and love of the honorable, but not iniquity or roguery—unless close association infects him with some vulgarity or error, like as flux or unwitting contact might infect an eye. So Plato's familiars, they say, imitated his stoop, Aristotle's his lisp, King Alexander's the angle of his neck and the roughness of his voice in conversation. People generally adopt the idiosyncrasies of others without being aware of it, but the flatterer's case is precisely the chameleon's. That creature can transform itself to every color except white; the flatterer cannot assimilate himself to any meritorious quality and therefore tries to imitate every bad quality there is. Like bad painters who are incapable of achieving beauty and so use wrinkles and warts and scars to effect a likeness, so the flatterer is an imitator of intemperance, superstition, irascibility, severity to servants, distrust of his household and relations. He himself has a natural propensity to the worse, and would seem very far from reproving the shameful conduct he imitates. It is those who strive for the better and show vexation and annoyance at their friends' derelictions who are suspected. It is this which made Dionysius suspicious of Dion, Philip of Samius, Ptolemy of Cleomenes, and ruined them. But the man who is and wishes to seem at once agreeable and loyal simulates greater satisfaction in worse conduct, as though his deep affection prevented him from taking exception to even vile behavior, because he has grown to share your character and reactions in every detail.

That is why flatterers insist on sharing even our involuntary and incidental peculiarities; when they court a sick man they pretend to have his disease, and to be unable to see or hear distinctly when they are in the company of the half-blind or half-deaf. The flatterers of Dionysius, whose vision was poor, used to stumble against each other and knock the dishes off the table at dinner. Some exploit their victims' mischances to get under their very skin, and blend their simulation with their victims' reactions even in matters unmentionable. If they discover that a man's marriage is unhappy or that he looks askance at his children or kindred, they give themselves without stint to lamenting about their own children or wives or kindred or household and catalogue their secret failings. Such similarity of experience creates a stronger bond of sympathy; the recipient of confidences divulges his own secrets and having done so falls into an intimacy for fear of a betrayal of trust. I myself know of a man who turned his wife out because his friend had divorced his; it was discovered, by the divorcée who was privy to the intrigue, that he paid secret visits to his wife and sent her messages. The inexperienced interpret the iambic description of a crab—

> Body nothing but belly, eyes that squint
> Every which way, a beast using teeth to creep on—

as referring to a flatterer; the picture is really of mere parasites, "stewpot and comestible friends" in Eupolis' phrase.

This topic, however, we shall postpone to its proper place in our discourse, but there is another dextrous simulation the flatterer practices which we must not pass over. If he imitates any of his victim's *good* qualities, the flatterer is careful to be outdistanced. Among true friends there is neither rivalry nor envy of one another; whether their success is equal or inferior they are unpained and unconcerned. But the flatterer always keeps it in mind that his is the supporting role and therefore purposely falls short of equality in his acting, acknowledging that he is outdone and outdistanced in everything except badness. But in badness he does not yield primacy: if his victim is out of sorts he declares that he himself is melancholy; if his victim is superstitious he is fanatic; if his victim is in love he is distracted. "You laughed out of turn," he says, "but I died laughing." But in good qualities he follows the opposite course. He says that he is a fast runner but his victim flies, that he is a tolerable horseman, "but nothing compared to a centaur like you. I have a talent for poetry and my lines are not bad but 'Not mine the thunder; it is Zeus's.' " By imitating his victim's tastes he seeks to show that they are good, and by allowing himself to be worsted that his prowess is incomparable. These then are the differences between flatterer and friend in respect to the assimilation of one to the other.

Let us now differentiate between them in another respect. We have remarked that the factor of pleasure is common to both—a good man takes as much pleasure in his friends as a bad man in his flatterers; we can define the difference by referring to the object of the pleasure. Consider: perfume has a fragrance and so has medicine; the difference is that the object of one is pleasure and nothing else, the object of the other is to purge or stimulate or add weight, with fragrance only incidental. Again, painters mix flowery colors and dyes, and some medical compounds too show agreeable colors and flowery tints. What is the difference? Is not the criterion obviously the object? In like manner the charm of friendship has, in addition to beauty and use, an extra bloom; there are times when friends play and eat and drink and, by Zeus, laugh and act the fool with one another, using these diversions as a sauce for weighty and serious matters. This is the meaning of such lines as "In talk they took their pleasure, together conversing" [*Iliad* 11.643], and, "Us nothing could part, in our love and mutual delight" [*Odyssey* 4.178]. But the aim and object of the flatterer's enterprise is always to cook up some spicy drollery or practical joke whose sole motive and end is pleasure. In a word, the flatterer will do anything at all to be agreeable, the friend will do what he ought. Sometimes this is agreeable and sometimes not, not because he wishes to be disagreeable but not evading even the disagreeable if it is for the best. He is like a physician who will prescribe saffron and nard if it will benefit, and sometimes, by Zeus, give soothing baths and a generous diet, but there are times when he disregards such things, doses a patient with castor or "Acrid polium, whose smell is most evil" [Nicander, *Theriaca* 64], or grind hellebore up and make him drink it down. His object, in one case as in the other, is not the agreeable or disagreeable, but in both solely conducive to a cure. So there are times when a friend guides a man towards goodness by complimenting him and gladdening him with courteous praise, like this:

> Teucer, dear man, Telamon's son and lord of your people,
> Well-shot, keep it up!   [*Iliad* 8.281]

or, "How could I ever forget god-like Odysseus?"
                                            [*Iliad* 10.243]

But when there is need of correction he belabors him with biting language and the outspokenness of a guardian:

> Menelaus, Zeus' ward, you are mad; you ought not
> Be so foolish.   [*Iliad* 7.109]

There are times when he seconds words with actions, as did Menedemus who brought the debauched and wanton son of his friend Asclepiades to his senses by closing the door upon him and not speaking to him. Arcesilaus forbade Battus his school because he had abused Cleanthes in a line of his comedy, and was reconciled only when Battus apologized to Cleanthes and placated him. To help a friend it is proper to hurt him, not that the hurt should rupture friendship, but to serve, like an astringent drug, to restore and preserve the patient. Like a musician who produces noble and salutary effects by the change, a friend now loosens his strings and now tightens them; frequently he is agreeable, he is helpful always. But the flatterer is always keyed to the same sweet note to make himself agreeable; he knows nothing of counterpoint or of a jarring word but can only follow another's will by joining him in melody and pitch. Xenophon tells us that Agesilaus welcomed praise from people capable of dispraising; so ought we regard commendations and courtesies as friendly only if the commender is also capable of pricking us on occasion and opposing us. But an association aimed solely at being agreeable, consistently bland and with complaisance unqualified, we must suspect. It is well, by Zeus, to keep that Spartan's remark handy; he said, when King Charillus was being commended, "How can he be a good man when he is not severe even with rogues?"

It is in the ear of the bull that the gadfly takes shelter, men say, and the tick in the ear of the dog. So the flatterer pre-empts the ears of ambitious men with praise and becomes so closely attached that he is hard to shake off. Here especially, then, we must be vigilant and alert to observe whether the praise is for the action or the man. It is for the action if they praise a man behind his back rather than in his presence, if they too aspire to and emulate the same conduct and praise it in others as well as in us, if they do not vacillate by doing and saying one thing at one time and the opposite at another, and most of all if we ourselves are sure that we do not regret and are not ashamed of the conduct for which we have been praised and do not wish that they had done or said the opposite. For if our own inner judgment protests and refuses to accept the praise then it is unaffected and impervious and impregnable to flattery. But somehow or other the greater part of humanity reject comforting thoughts in adversity but are susceptible to those who join them in deploring and lamenting. When they have erred or offended, the man who causes them to rue what they have done by sharp chiding and reproof they regard as an enemy and adversary; but they welcome the man who praises and felicitates them on their action and count him well disposed and a friend.

People who give easy praise and applause to any deed or word, serious or frivolous, are hurtful only for the moment, while the incident is in progress. But when their praises penetrate to his natural disposition and their flattery affects his very character, by Zeus, then they are like thieving servants who filch not from the granary but from the seed. Disposition and character are the seed of conduct, and by clothing vice with the titles of virtue they subvert life's very source and fountain. Thucydides [3.82] tells us that during revolutions and wars "words had to change their ordinary meaning and to take that which was now given them. Reckless audacity came to be considered the courage of a loyal ally; prudent hesitation, specious cowardice; moderation was held to be a cloak for unmanliness; ability to see all sides of a question inaptness to act on any." In the case of flattery too we must diligently beware of profligacy being called liberality, cowardice wariness, recklessness gallantry, stinginess frugality, amorousness sociability and amiability, irascibility and arrogance manliness, insignificance and lowliness charity. Plato somewhere remarks [*Republic* 474 e] that the lover (who is his beloved's flatterer) calls a snub nose cute, a hawk nose royal, brunettes virile, blonds children of the gods; "honey-pale" he says is the coinage of a lover who cheerfully tolerates a greenish complexion and gives it a pet name.

Now an ugly man who is persuaded that he is handsome or a short man that he is tall will not long stay deceived, and the harm done him is slight and not irreparable. But the praise which habituates a man not to be troubled by vices but to rejoice in them as if they were virtues, which banishes shame for misdeeds, is ruinous. It crushed the Sicilians by calling Dionysius' and Phalaris' bloodthirstiness "impatience with villainy"; it destroyed Egypt by styling Ptolemy's womanishness and fanaticism and hallelujahs and banging tambourines "piety" and "worship of the gods." It almost succeeded in toppling and erasing Roman character by extenuating Anthony's voluptuousness and wantonness and sumptuous displays as the affable and charitable conduct of a gentleman generously favored by power and fortune. What else made Ptolemy the perennial piper, or set a tragic stage for Nero and fitted him with masks and buskins? Was it not the praise of flatterers? Are not kings generally hailed as Apollos if they hum a tune, Dionysuses if they tipple, Heracleses if they wrestle, and does not gratification at this flattery lead them to every sort of unseemliness?

We must therefore be on particular guard when the flatterer is at his praises. He himself is aware of this and is deft in parrying suspicion. If he gets hold of some dude or of a yokel wearing a rawhide smock, he indulges all his snottiness, like Strouthias in the play who tramples over Bias and dances a jig on his doltishness by praising him in such a line as "You have outdrunk King Alexander," or "So funny, that business with the Cyprian!" But when he notices that people are better brushed in this department, on to his ways and guarding the fortress and its approaches, he does not march his praise for a direct assault but wheels about in a long detour, advancing silently to make contact and tempt his quarry like some woodland creature. Now he reports laudatory remarks "others" have made, alleging some third party as orators do when they "quote," and saying how pleased he was to meet with certain strangers or elders in the market place who admired him so much and had so many good things to say about him. Again he will cook up some insignificant and baseless charge which he pretends he heard from others and then bustles up to ask when he could have said or done such a thing. His victim naturally enters a denial, whereupon he makes the man a sitting duck for his volley of praise. "I was astonished at your speaking ill of friends when it is not in your nature to speak ill even of enemies, and at your reaching for others' property when you give away so much of your own."

Others are like painters who emphasize bright and luminous areas by shadowy and somber backgrounds. They surreptitiously praise and coddle the vices characteristic of their victims by reprehending and condemning their opposites or traducing and ridiculing them. Frugality they disparage as rusticity when their victims are dissolute, and when they are greedy rogues who grow rich on disgraceful and wicked doings they malign contentment and honesty as timorousness and feebleness in doing business. When they fall in with easy-tempered do-nothings who avoid the bustle of the city they are not ashamed to call civic duty tiresome meddling and ambition fruitless vainglory. To flatter an orator they sneer at a philosopher, and they stand well with wanton women by referring to faithful and devoted wives as frigid and provincial. Villainy outdoes itself when the flatterers do not spare even themselves. Just as wrestlers assume a low stance in order to throw their opponents, so by criticizing themselves the flatterers wriggle into position for admiring their victim. "I am a lily-livered slave at sea," he says, "I resign when the going is hard. I go crazy mad when I am ill-spoken of; but this man finds nothing terrifying, nothing hard. He is a peculiar type; nothing fazes him, nothing irks him."

The expert flatterer does not use this approach but has a different technique for the man who imagines that he is very brainy and chooses to be forthright and independent, who always advertises his uprightness by quoting, "Do not praise me to excess, Diomede, and do not chide me" [*Iliad* 10.249]. Such a man the flatterer approaches, as a man obviously superior, to ask advice on private matters, saying that he does have more intimate friends but feels obliged to trouble him. "Where can folk who want counsel find help? Whom can a man trust?" And when he has heard what the man has to say he goes off declaring that he had got not counsel but an oracle. If he sees that the man prides himself on proficiency in literature he gives him some of his own writing and begs him to read and correct it. King Mithridates was an amateur doctor, and some of his companions let him practice surgery and cautery on them —that was flattery indeed, and not only in word, for their trust seemed to certify his proficiency. "The divine assumes many forms," and this species of self-denying praise which requires a cunning kind of precaution can be unmasked by purposely making your advice and suggestions absurd and your corrections silly. If he never takes exception, if he nods confirmation to everything and accepts everything and cries, "Excellent, bravo!" at every point, then clearly his wish is to praise and puff up; "His request is for the password, his object other."

There is also a kind of praise which is silent flattery, just as painting, according to certain critics, is silent poetry. Hunters are less likely to be suspected by their quarry if they appear not to be hunters but travelers or shepherds or tillers; so flatterers too find a target for their praises when they seem not to be praising but doing something else. By yielding his chair or his couch to a newcomer, by breaking off in the middle of a speech to the assembly or senate when he notices that some nabob wishes to speak and giving up the floor along with his speech, his silence proclaims louder than a shout that he regards the nabob as the better man and outstandingly wise. That is why one can see such people occupying the front seats at recitals and theaters; it is not because they suppose they deserve them, but in order to flatter the rich by giving them up. At meetings and deliberations they start a line of argument and then yield as if in deference to their betters and readily shift to the opposition if the speaker on the other side is powerful or rich or famous. This, then, is the appropriate test for unmasking such cringing and submissiveness: they yield not to experience or virtue or age but to wealth and reputation.

Megabyzus sat down by the painter Apelles and chose to babble about lines and shadows, whereupon Apelles said: "Do you see the apprentices there grinding pigments? When you kept quiet they paid careful attention to you and admired your purple and gold, but now they are laughing at you for undertaking to speak about things you have never learned about." And Solon, when Croesus questioned him on happiness, declared that an obscure Athenian named Tellus and the brothers Cleobis and Biton had a happier fate. But flatterers hail kings and millionaires and rulers not only as fortunate and blessed but also as peerless in intelligence and craftsmanship and every good quality.

Some will not abide to hear the Stoics call the sage at once rich, handsome, well born, and a king, but flatterers insist that the rich man is at once an orator and a poet, and if he would have it so, a painter and a piper, and swift and strong. They take a fall when they wrestle with their victim and lag behind when they race, as Crison of Himera did when he was running against Alexander; but Alexander was indignant when he found out. Carneades used to say that the sons of millionaires and kings learned only to ride, but nothing else well and truly, for at their studies their teachers flatter them with praise and their wrestling partners lose by design; but a horse does not know or care who is commoner or king, rich or poor, and throws anyone who cannot ride him. Bion's comment is therefore silly and ridiculous: "If a man were going to make a field fertile and fruitful by praising it, would he not appear to be in the wrong if he failed to do so but bothered with it and tilled it? Nor is it amiss for a man to be praised if praise alone can make him useful and productive." But a field does not become worse when it is praised, whereas those who praise a man falsely and beyond his merit puff him up and ruin him.

So much, then, for the topic of praise; next we must examine the topic of outspokenness. When Patroclus accoutered himself in Achilles' armor and drove his horses forth to battle he did not venture to lay hands on the Pelian spear but left it behind; so the flatterer when he equips himself with the counterfeit insignia and heraldic devices of friendship ought to leave behind, without fingering or imitating it, the weapon of outspokenness, "heavy and huge and mighty," which only friendship can wield. But to avoid being recognized for what they are by their jokes and japes and antics and frivolity, the flatterers now address themselves to their business with knitted brow and frowningly mingle reproach and admonition with their flattery; we must therefore include this aspect in our examination.

The sham Heracles comes on, in Menander's comedy, carrying a club which is not solid and strong, but a soft and hollow imitation; similarly, I think, if we try the flatterer's outspokenness it will prove to be soft and light and flabby, like women's cushions which seem to bolster the head and give it solid support but in fact yield to pressure and flatten out. That spurious outspokenness with its empty and false and stage-prop bulk is similarly puffed out and made impressive, so that when it contracts and collapses it creates a vacuum to pull down any that puts his weight upon it. The true outspokenness of a friend cleaves to failings and its prick is solicitous and salutary; it is like honey, which stings as it cleanses a wound but is beneficial and sweet in other respects. We shall deal with this in the sequel.

In the first place, the flatterer affects a stern and harsh

and inexorable attitude in his dealings with others. He is
severe with his slaves, alert to castigate the failings of his
relatives and household, never admires or respects but
always looks down on others, an implacable prosecutor
who whets other people's anger, in quest of a reputation
as a puritan who would not temper his outspokenness for
anyone or do or say anything to make himself agreeable.
In the second place, he pretends not to be aware of or
notice actual and important faults, but is alert to pounce
upon petty and irrelevant failings; he will belabor a man
most vehemently and emphatically if he sees that his
furniture is carelessly placed, his housekeeping is ineffi-
cient, his hair untrimmed and his coat carelessly draped,
his horse or dog negligently groomed. But slighting parents, neglecting children, insulting one's wife, scorning
one's household, squandering one's money, are outside his
range; here he is mute and spineless, like a trainer who
lets an athlete go drinking and wenching but is very strict
about oil flask and scraper, or a schoolmaster who scolds
a boy about his tablet and stylus and pretends not to hear
his solecisms and barbarisms. The flatterer is the sort of
man who has nothing to say about the argument of a
cheap and ridiculous speaker but finds fault with his
voice and criticizes him sharply for ruining his throat by
drinking cold water, or who, when he is asked to go over
some miserable screed, will find fault with the coarseness
of the paper and call the scribe a careless wretch. So the
flatterers of Ptolemy, who fancied himself a scholar, fought
with him about a word or a line or a story and kept it up
half the night; but not one of them took a stand when
Ptolemy was cruel or outrageous, when he banged his
tambourine or enacted his initiations. For flatterers to
apply outspokenness only to parts that do no harm and
give no pain is precisely like using a surgeon's scalpel
to trim a man's hair or pare his nails when he is suffering
from fistulas and abscesses.

But there are some yet more villainous who employ
outspokenness and chiding to give pleasure. For instance,
when Alexander gave large gifts to a certain jester, Agis
the Argive was moved by envy and chagrin to cry out,

"What awful absurdity!" The king turned to him angrily and said, "What's that you say?" "I must confess," he replied, "that I am irked and irritated when I see all you sons of Zeus alike take pleasure in flatterers and clowns. Heracles was amused by those Cercopes and Dionysus by Silenuses, and you too obviously prize such fellows." Once when Tiberius Caesar entered the senate one of the flatterers arose and declared that they ought to speak out, like the free men they were, and not brush aside or turn a blind eye to business of public interest. This preamble excited attention, and when all had fallen silent and Tiberius was listening, he said: "Hear, Caesar, the complaint which we all have against you but which no one has the courage to proffer openly. You are careless of yourself, you squander your energy and wear yourself out in constant anxiety and toil in our behalf, and you never take a rest day or night." As he prated on in this same vein the orator Cassius Severus remarked, it is said, "That man's outspokenness will be the death of him!"

But this is only a trifle. It becomes serious when the flatterers chide a man for passions and failings which are the reverse of those he labors under; this can be hurtful to the foolish. For example, the flatterer Himerius used to scold a rich Athenian who was extremely stingy and avaricious for being an extravagant spendthrift bound to starve to death with his children. Or they will scold profligate spendthrifts as penurious and drab (as Titus Petronius did Nero); or bid savage and cruel rulers to lay aside their excessive moderation and their unseasonable and profitless pity for their subjects. Of the same stripe is the man who pretends to be on guard against some simple and feckless fool and to fear him as a shrewd rogue. Or if some malicious fellow whose pleasure is always to malign and find fault is ever brought to praise some illustrious figure, this kind of flatterer will assail him and reprove his weakness in praising people nothing worth. "Who is this fellow and what has he said or done that is so brilliant?"

Where love is involved flatterers are especially active and add fuel to their victims' flames. When they see brothers at odds or children despising their parents or husbands jealous of their wives, they do not admonish or blame them but exacerbate their irritation. "You do not realize your value," they say, or, "It is your fault; you always make yourself servile and humble." But if it is a courtesan or an adulterous paramour the man is annoyed with, because of a fit of temper or jealousy, the flatterer is on the spot with his splendid outspokenness, heaping fire on fire, playing the advocate, charging the lover with much unloverlike, hard, and culpable behavior. "Ah, ingrate, those close kisses!"

When Antony was burning with love for his Egyptian, his friends urged that the woman doted on him and scolded him for being unfeeling and haughty. "The woman has abandoned high royalty with its pomp and luxury and is wearing herself out campaigning with you like some camp follower. 'Adamant is the mind within you' [*Odyssey* 10. 329], and you are indifferent to her anguish." Being arraigned as the offender pleased Antony, and he was more charmed with the upbraiding than he could ever be with praise, quite unaware that the seeming admonition was but an added snare. Outspokenness like this is like the biting of wanton women: it tickles and titillates to voluptuousness by seeming to hurt. Neat wine by itself is an antidote for hemlock, but if it is put into a blend with hemlock, the force of the poison is irresistible, for the heat carries it to the heart at once. So scoundrels who understand that outspokenness is a powerful antidote against flattery use outspokenness itself for their flattery. Bias' answer to the man who asked what animal is most hurtful is therefore incomplete. His answer was, "Of wild animals the tyrant, of tame the flatterer." It were truer to say that of flatterers those who ply bath and table are tame, but one who spreads his meddling and slander and mischief tentacle-like into bedrooms and women's corridors is wild and savage and most intractable.

Here is one likely mode of defense. Know and always bear in mind that the soul contains on the one hand truth and honor and rationality, and on the other unreason and falsehood and passion. A friend is always ready to counsel and promote the better, like a physician who preserves and enlarges what is sound; but the flatterer supports the passionate and irrational part, which he tickles and titillates and cajoles, and he devises disreputable pleasures for it to set it against the rational part. There are certain dishes which do not assimilate to blood or breath and contribute nothing to sinews or marrow but only agitate the genitals and excite the belly and produce unwholesome and flabby flesh. So the flatterer's conversation adds nothing to reasoning or intelligence but only facilitates voluptuous love, intensifies some senseless temper, stimulates envy, inflates an empty and offensive conceit, increases lamentation in grief, accentuates mischief and illiberality and distrust by calumnies and premonitions to create hostility and fear and suspicion. The heedful will be aware of his effects. Always he lurks for some passion, which he then fattens up; he is like a pustule, and appears as an abscessed or inflamed spot in the soul. "Are you angry? Punish! Do you covet? Buy! Are you afraid? Let's run! Do you suspect? Believe!"

In these passions it may be difficult to detect the flatterer because their magnitude and intensity militate against reason; but in lesser emotions he offers more of a holdfast, for his procedure is the same. If, for example, a man is apprehensive of a hang-over or surfeit and therefore hesitant about bathing or eating, a friend will restrain him and advise him to watch his step and be careful, but the flatterer drags him to the baths, insists that he be served with some strange dish, and tells him not to mortify his flesh by abstinence. And if he notices that a man is inclined to shirk a journey or a voyage or some piece of business he will say there's no hurry: the result would be the same if he put it off, or he could get a proxy to act for him. If a man has promised to lend or give money to some close connection and is hovering between regret and shame, the flatterer adds his weight to the worse scale, reinforces the man's tenderness for his purse, cuts away his sense of shame, and enjoins thrift on the grounds that he has many expenses and is responsible for supporting a large family. It follows that if we recognize our own greed and shamelessness and inconstancy we shall also recognize the flatterer, for he is always the patron of these passions and openly advocates indulging them. But enough of this.

We must now proceed to the question of assistance and service. Here the flatterer succeeds in creating perplexity and ambiguity, for his apparent diligence, alacrity, and dependability make it hard to distinguish him from a friend. The character of a friend is what Euripides called the language of truth—"simple, natural, and unvarnished," whereas the flatterer's is truly "Diseased to the core, in need of wise cures" [Euripides, *Phoenician Women* 469 ff.]—many cures, by Zeus, and passing wise. Take a chance meeting: sometimes without a word said or heard a friend gives and receives indications of sincere good will and affection at a glance and then passes on. But the flatterer pursues you at a run and hails you at a distance, and if it happens that you saw and greeted him first he apologizes on oath and produces witnesses that he did not see you. It is the same with polite services: friends omit trivialities, are not punctilious and officious, and do not thrust themselves forward for every kind of service. But the flatterer is persistent and unremitting and indefatigable; he leaves no one else place or opportunity to assist, but is eager for orders, and if he receives none he is peeved or rather cast down to earth and howls for grief. To sensible people these are symptoms not of genuine and sober friendship but of harlotry too ready for close embraces.

But we must first examine the differences in their advertisement. Our predecessors have rightly observed that a friend's tender is like this: "If I can, if it is a thing that can be accomplished" [*Iliad* 14.196]; whereas a flatterer's is like this: "Speak what is in your mind" [*Iliad* 14.195]. It is the comic poets who introduce characters like this:

> Match me with that soldier, Nicomachus.
> I'll reduce him to jelly, I'll scourge him,
> I'll make his face more porous than a sponge.

In the second place, no friend will cooperate unless he has first been consulted, and only after he has scrutinized the project and has helped set it on a decent and advantageous footing. But the flatterer is not only eager to yield and oblige but also dreads giving an impression of being reluctant and loath to undertake the work, and, therefore, even if he is given the opportunity to join in scrutinizing the project and pronouncing upon it, he is obsequious to the other's desire and eggs him on. There are very few rich men or princes who will say:

> Would I had a beggar, aye worse than a beggar,
> Who would speak his heart for mine own good,
> Oblivious to fear.

It is a chorus of friends they want, like tragic actors, or an applauding audience. That is why Merope in the tragedy utters this admonition:

> Get you friends not obsequious in speech,
> But rogues complaisant to your pleasure
> Bar and bolt out of your house.

But people do the reverse. "The friends not obsequious in speech" who oppose them for their own good are anathema; "the rogues complaisant," the toadies and impostors, they not only welcome within "bar and bolt of the house" but within their inmost feelings and secrets. The simpler sort of flatterer does not think he need or ought be consulted in such matters but only that he be the minister and tool. But the more accomplished rogue takes his stand where the problem is being mooted, knits his brows, makes the appropriate grimaces, and says nothing; then when the other expresses his view he cries, "By Heracles! You took the words out of my mouth! I was just going to say the same thing." Surfaces and lines, say the mathematicians, do not bend or extend or move, for they are without body and imaginary; they bend or extend or move along with the bodies whose extremities they are. So you shall detect the flatterer by his similar dependence in word and expression, and, by Zeus, in pleasure and anger. In these respects the difference between flatterer and friend is easy to detect.

It is even easier in the mode of his services. A favor done by a friend keeps its essential force deep within, like a living creature; there is no superficial display or ostentation. Like a doctor who cures without his patient's knowledge, so a friend's solicitude is frequently effective without its object's knowledge, as when he speaks to someone on his behalf or resolves a misunderstanding. Arcesilaus was that kind of friend. Among other instances was his kindness to Apelles the Chian when he was sick. When Arcesilaus saw how poor he was he brought twenty drachmas on his next visit and said, as he sat by Apelles, "There is nothing here but Empedocles' elements—'Fire, water, earth, and gentle ether on high.' Your bed is not even well made." So saying he rearranged his pillow and put the money underneath. When his old serving-woman found it and with astonishment told Apelles, he said, with a smile, "This is a piece of Arcesilaus' thievery."

"Children favor their fathers" is true in philosophy too. When Cephisocrates was defendant in a suit, Arcesilaus' acquaintance Lacydes, with other friends, came to his support. The prosecutor asked Cephisocrates for his ring, whereupon he quietly dropped it and Lacydes, who was watching him, stepped on it and hid it. The issue depended on the ring. One of the jurors, it seems, noticed what had happened, and when Cephisocrates was paying his respects to the jury after the verdict, he bade him thank Lacydes and then told the whole story, but Lacydes never told anyone. The gods too, I believe, keep most of their benefactions secret, for it is in their nature to take satisfaction in conferring favors and benefits.

But the flatterer's enterprise has no whit of integrity or truth or simplicity or ingenuousness but only sweat and noise and bustle and a harried look to enhance the impression of the intense effort he is devoting to your interests. He is like an overwrought painting which aims at striking the imagination with garish pigments and exaggerated drapery and wrinkles and angularity. He gives tiresome explanations of the trips he has had to make, the worries he has had, the people he has had to disoblige; and he details the enormous and infinite trouble he has taken. The natural response is that the business was not worth all the bother; any service for which too much credit is claimed becomes displeasing and burdensome and intolerable, and in the flatterer's case the dissatisfaction and vexation is not put off to a later time but is felt while his work is in progress. But a friend reports his deed modestly, if he must speak of it, and says nothing about himself. That is how the Lacedaemonians behaved when they sent food to relieve a famine in Smyrna. When the appreciative Smyrnaeans extolled them, they said, "It was no great matter; we collected the shipment by voting that we and our cattle go without lunch for one day." Such courtesy is not only well bred but also more acceptable to the recipients, for they can imagine that their benefactors suffered no great deprivation.

But it is not in the importunity of his services or in his readiness to undertake them that the character of the flatterer is best recognized; a better gauge is whether his assistance is honorable or indecent, and whether its object is pleasure or utility. A friend will not, as Gorgias has him do, claim his friend's assistance in honest enterprises and in return himself assist in many that are dishonest. "To share prudence, not folly, is his nature" [Euripides, *Iphigenia at Aulis* 407]. Rather will he deflect his friend from unseemly courses. And if he cannot sway him, Phocion's retort to Antipater is apt: "You cannot use me as both friend and flatterer"—which is to say, as friend and as non-friend. We must cooperate with a friend's endeavors but not his knaveries, his plans but not his conspiracies, his testimony but not his deceptions, his ups and downs, by Zeus, but not his dishonesty. We should not choose even to be conscious of a friend's derelictions: how can we choose to be his accomplice and partner in his iniquity? When the Lacedaemonians were treating with Antipater after he defeated them in battle they asked him to penalize them any way he liked but not to impose terms that were dishonorable. Similarly, a friend will be the first to insist on being called upon and eager to do his part without offering excuses if some need arises which involves expense and risk and effort, but where knavery is involved he will beg off and obtain his dismissal. But flattery, on the other hand, abdicates where a service involves hardship and danger; if you rap on him to test him, he will produce an impure sound, muddled with excuses. Use him for a villainous or vile or disreputable errand, trample upon him, he will not think it extraordinary or take affront.

Consider the monkey. He cannot watch the house like a dog, he cannot carry like a horse, he cannot plow a field like an ox; and therefore he bears insult and is the butt for buffoonery and ridicule. The flatterer, similarly, cannot plead for you or share an expense or espouse your quarrel because he is incapable of any exertion and any serious business, and so he never demurs at any underhanded commission; he is a trustworthy pander for lust, expert in paying a prostitute off, meticulous in totting up the bill for wine, no sluggard in arranging a supper, attentive to courtesans; but if you commission him to be sharp with your in-laws or to help get rid of your wife he is merciless and brazen. Here too, then, the man is not hard to detect; if he is assigned any disreputable and repulsive task you like he is ready to give himself unsparingly to make himself agreeable to his principal.

Their attitude to your other friends is a major criterion; here you can perceive a great difference between flatterer and friend. To a friend it is most sweet to love and be loved along with many others, and he is sedulous to have his friend have many friends and be much prized. Believing that friends share resources, he thinks that friends above all are the resource to be shared. But the flatterer is false and supposititious and adulterated, for he knows that he is debasing friendship as if he were counterfeiting a coin. He is naturally jealous, but he directs his jealousy to his own guild, competing to outdo them in buffoonery and babbling. Before his betters he cringes and quakes, not, by Zeus, like "Infantryman marching by Lydian chariot," but, as Simonides says, "With no lead even to put beside pure molten gold." Being light and meretricious and deceptive, therefore, when he is tested beside genuine and massive and solid friendship, the flatterer cannot stand the examination and does what the man who painted a wretched picture of cocks did. He ordered his servant to shoo all real cocks away from his canvas; and so the flatterer shoos all real friends away and won't let them come near. If he cannot, he openly fawns upon them and is obsequious to them and shows them the attentions due superiors, but secretly he sows and plants slander. When his secret gossip has chafed and made a sore but without accomplishing its purpose, he remembers and acts upon Medius' rule. This Medius was the expert choir leader who gave the pitch to the chorus of flatterers who surrounded Alexander and stood shoulder to shoulder against good men. He bade them lay on boldly with their slanders and bite deep, explaining that even if the tooth marks cicatrized the scar would remain. It was by such scars, indeed, or rather by such gangrene and ulcers that Alexander was devoured and so destroyed Callisthenes and Parmenio and Philotas and committed himself unreservedly to be tripped up by the Hagnos, Bagoases, Agesiases, and Demetriuses; they bedizened him and transformed him into a heathen idol to be groveled to. So great is the power of catering to gratification, and greatest, it seems, with men that cut the greatest figure. Their own noble conceptions and aspirations give the flatterer encouragement and confidence. Terrain that is lofty is hard for an assailant to approach or encompass, but a lofty temperament in a soul which is heedless because of the endowments of nature or Fortune is easily accessible to puny and lowly aggressors.

I therefore repeat what I urged at the beginning of this discourse: we must banish self-love and conceit. It is our antecedent self-flattery which softens us up and prepares us to receive flattery from without. But we shall not readily offer ourselves to be trodden over by flatterers if we hearken to the god and understand the high value of "Know thyself" to each of us, if we reflect upon our character and upbringing and education and realize how numberless are our lapses from excellence and how inextricably blended they are with badness and heedlessness in deeds and words and emotions. Alexander declared that his propensity to sleep and to love made him disbelieve those who proclaimed him a god, on the grounds that these propensities revealed a lack of nobility and an excess of passion. We too, if we survey our numerous and varied lapses, ugly or regrettable, our failings and our faults, shall discover that what we need is a friend not to praise and eulogize us but to reprove and be outspoken and scold, by Zeus, if we behave badly. Only a small minority have courage enough to speak plainly to a friend rather than say something agreeable, and in this minority it is rare to find any that understand how it should be done; they mistake railing and abuse for outspokenness. But like any other medicine, outspokenness administered at an inappropriate time only causes useless pain and agitation, and, in a manner of speaking, achieves no more by giving pain than flattery does by giving pleasure. Unseasonable blame is no less harmful than unseasonable praise. It lays its object wide open to the flatterer's attack, for he will react like water which glides away from uphill obstacles down to low and inviting valleys. Outspokenness must therefore be diluted with courtesy; it stands to reason that its excess and concentration should be mitigated as we do a glare, so that people should not be so disturbed and distressed by being reprimanded and rebuked at every turn that they look about for something painless and fly for refuge to the flatterer's shade.

The proper corrective for any vice, Philopappus, is virtue, not polarization of the vice. Some people suppose that the corrective for bashfulness is impudence, for country breeding being a smart aleck, and make the furthest remove from timidity and effeminacy an approach to swashbuckling and rodomontade. Some substitute atheism for superstition and rascality for naïveté; like men who do not know how to straighten a stick, they force the crookedness in their character from one direction to the other. Giving needless pain is an ugly disavowal of flattery. To avoid the imputation of vulgarity and lowliness in friendship by being harsh and disagreeable argues a gauche and uncivilized inconsiderateness. An ex-slave on the comic stage thinks railing is freedom of speech.

It is an ugly thing, then, for the desire to be agreeable to degenerate into flattery, and it is ugly too when eschewing flattery leads to spoiling friendly solicitude by unbridled outspokenness. Our proper course is to err in neither direction but to find the norm for outspokenness, as for everything else, in the mean.

The development that this topic seems to call for will put the finishing touch on this composition. Seeing that sundry blemishes adhere to outspokenness, let us first rid it of self-love and take great care that our reprimands shall not seem to be motivated by some personal resentment of an injury or the like. A man speaking in his own interest is thought to be actuated not by kindness but by passion, and his criticism passes for faultfinding rather than admonition. Admonition is friendly and large spirited, faultfinding selfish and petty, and it follows that men respect and admire those that speak out but recriminate and condemn faultfinders. Agamemnon could not brook Achilles' apparently moderate outspokenness, but tolerated and yielded to Odysseus' bitter invective—

> You disaster! Would you ruled some other,
> Some poltroon army!
>
> [*Iliad* 14.84]

—containing himself because the chiding was responsible and reasonable. Odysseus had no ground for personal vindictiveness but spoke out on behalf of Greece, whereas Achilles seemed to be angry for personal reasons. And Achilles himself, not a man "with sweetness in his heart and kindly" but "a terrible man capable of blaming the blameless," silently submitted when Patroclus inveighed against him—

> Pitiless! Knightly Peleus was never your father
> Nor Thetis your mother; it was the gray sea that bore you
> And craggy rocks, so adamant is your heart.
>
> [*Iliad* 16.33 ff.]

The orator Hypereides used to ask the Athenians to consider not merely whether he was bitter but whether he was bitter for naught; so a friend's admonition, if it is untainted by personal passion, inspires respect and veneration and shamefastness. The tenor of outspokenness is irresistible if the speaker makes it clear that he is waiving and totally disregarding his friend's derelictions towards himself, and that he is chiding him for other offenses and goading him unmercifully on behalf of others; the admonisher's sweetness of temper gives sharper pungency and edge to his admonition.

When we are at odds with our friends and annoyed with them, it has been said, is precisely the time for us to safeguard and act for their interest and honor. That is true, but it is no less the part of a friend, when he feels himself overlooked and neglected, to speak out and call to mind others who are equally neglected. When Plato was in disgrace with Dionysius he asked the privilege of an interview, which Dionysius granted in the expectation that Plato would treat him to an inventory of grievances. But Plato's conversation ran somewhat as follows: "If you were informed, Dionysius, that an ill-willed person had sailed to Sicily intending to harm you but had found no opportunity to do so, would you let him get off with impunity and sail home again?" "Far from it, Plato," said Dionysius. "We must abhor and punish not only hostile acts but intentions as well." "Well then," said Plato, "a good-willed person has come here intending to benefit you in a certain way, and you have given him no opportunity to do so; is it right to let him go slighted and neglected?" When Dionysius asked who the man was, Plato answered, "Aeschines, a character as sterling as any of Socrates' company and effective in improving those with whom he converses. He has made the long voyage here to meet with you in philosophic discourse, but has been disregarded." This so moved Dionysius that he embraced Plato forthwith and made much of him, entranced by his benevolence and high-mindedness; and Aeschines was looked after honorably and handsomely.

Next, we must scour our outspokenness clean of every insult and ridicule and mockery and pertness and banish all invidious spicing. When a surgeon operates his hand should move swiftly with deft and clean strokes and eschew the superfluous leaps and vaults of a double-jointed ballet artiste. So outspokenness can tolerate apt and urbane phrases if such polish does not impair its gravity; but when brazenness and vulgarity and insult are injected its effect is canceled out and destroyed. Aptly and neatly did the fiddler close Philip's mouth when he tried to discuss pizzicato with him: "Heaven forfend Your Majesty should know these things better than I!" But Epicharmus' retort was too blunt. Hiero had done away with some of his friends, and a few days later invited Epicharmus to dinner. Said he, "But the other day friends sacrificing you did not invite." Antiphon's answer too was bad. When there was a discussion at Dionysius' on the question, "What sort of bronze is best?" Antiphon said, "The kind of which they molded the statues of [the tyrannicides] Harmodius and Aristogeiton at Athens." Such barbs and bitterness do no good, nor do pertness and sauciness give pleasure; such things are a species of malignant profligacy blended with mischief-making and highhandedness. People that indulge in it are simply dancing on the brink of the pit and must destroy themselves. Antiphon was killed by Dionysius, and Timagenes fell from Augustus Caesar's favor. Timagenes never uttered any liberal sentiment, but at every party and on every stroll he would say, with no serious purpose in view, "Any word he thought might amuse the Argives" [*Iliad* 2.215], alleging friendship as a cover for buffoonery.

The comic poets did, indeed, address sober and civic-minded observations to their audience, but their admixture of the ridiculous and the scurrilous spoiled their outspokenness and rendered it useless, like a bad sauce on food, so that their lines only gave the authors a reputation for mischief and vulgarity and did the hearers no good. There are times when playfulness and jokes may be brought to bear on friends, but outspokenness must retain its sobriety and its proper character. And if the issue be important, sincerity and attitude and tone of voice should carry conviction and arouse conscience.

Missing the proper moment is always disastrous, but it quite ruins the utility of outspokenness. Obviously it must be avoided when men are in their cups. To introduce at a gay and jolly party a discourse that wrinkles the brow and freezes the face is like obscuring a serene sky with a heavy cloud. It is tantamount to declaring war on Bacchus the Liberator, who, in Pindar's phrase, "loosens the coil of anxious care." Unseasonableness entails a great danger. Wine makes men's spirits teeter towards anger, and drunkenness, when it takes over, makes outspokenness enmity. In general, it is neither upstanding nor stouthearted but rather unmanly for a man who never speaks out on sober occasions to speak out when the flagons fly. That is the way of a cringing cur. But there is no need to expand on this.

Many people think it superfluous and presumptuous to regulate friends whose situation is flourishing, in the belief that success makes admonition irrelevant and futile; but when their friends stumble and fall they lay on and trample them in their subdued and humbled state, flooding them with reproof like a torrent which has broken its dam, gleeful at the transformation of their friend's former lordliness and their own impotence. It would not be amiss, therefore, to treat of this propensity also and to offer a reply to the question posed by Euripides [*Orestes* 667]: "What need of friends when our daimon vouchsafes prosperity?" It is when they are prosperous that men are most in need of friends who will speak out and bridle their extravagant fancies. Few indeed can combine prosperity with sobriety. Most require an injection of discretion from without, some external intelligence to restrain their waywardness when they are puffed out by Fortune. But when the daimon has cast a man down and stripped his grandeur away, his fall is in itself admonition and a call to repentance. Then is not the time for a friend's outspokenness or for grave and mordant lectures; then, when disaster has befallen, is it truly "Sweet to look into the eyes of a loyal comrade" [Euripides, *Ion* 732] who offers comfort and encouragement. When men embattled and imperiled saw Clearchus' kindly and benevolent face, Xenophon tells us, they faced danger with heightened courage. But to apply mordant outspokenness to a man in misfortune is like applying a stimulant to a distempered and inflamed eye; it neither cures nor relieves the pain, but only compounds it with the smart of anger and exacerbates the suffering. No man in good health will be at all annoyed or irritated with a friend who chides him for wenching and drinking, for his idleness and want of exercise, his constant bathing and unseasonable stuffing; but for a sick man to be told, "This is what comes of your intemperance, your indulgence, your dainties, your women," is intolerable and worse than the disease. "Man alive, what a time you choose! Here I am writing my will, the doctors are dosing me with castor and scammony, and you go preaching and philosophizing!" Adversity, you see, has no room for berating and copybook maxims; what it needs is gentleness and help. When little children fall nurses do not dash up to scold them, but they help them up and wash them and put them in order, and then reprimand or punish them.

A story is told of Demetrius of Phalerum when he had been banished from his country and was leading a humble and obscure existence near Thebes. Once he saw Crates making towards him, and squirmed in the expectation of a rough diatribe with characteristically Cynic outspokenness. But Crates' greeting was very gentle; he explained that exile entailed no evil and was not worth fretting over, but that it was rather a release from slippery and unstable preoccupations, and at the same time urged him to have confidence in himself and his situation. Demetrius was at once sweetened and took heart, and remarked to his friends: "Damn that busy scurrying! It has kept me from knowing a man like this."

> For the son of grief friendly words and jolly;
> But reproof for the man steeped in folly.

That is the character of well-bred friends.

But ill-bred and base flatterers of the well to do are "like old fractures and sprains," to use Demosthenes' language; "they stir to life whenever a mishap befalls the body." So such people are attached to catastrophe, as if they gloated over it. If a man does need to be reminded how his own indiscretion has brought him to grief it is enough to quote:

> Against our will was it done; for my part
> I urged against it strongly.
>
> [*Iliad* 9.108]

Where, then, is severity in place, when should a friend speak out with sternness? When circumstances suggest a brake upon voluptuousness or irascibility or highhandedness, when avarice needs to be checked or heedless folly restrained. An example is Solon's outspokenness to Croesus, who was corrupted and debilitated by mutable Fortune; Solon bade him look to his end. Another is Socrates' curb upon Alcibiades; his reproof brought actual tears to Alcibiades' eyes and turned his heart. Others are Cyrus' criticism of Cyaxares and Plato's of Dion. When Dion was in his heyday and turned all eyes upon himself by the beauty and grandeur of his works, Plato admonished him to watch himself and eschew "willfulness as a housemate of solitude." Speusippus also wrote Dion admonishing him not to be uplifted because there was much talk of him among women and children but to see to it that Sicily should be adorned with holiness and justice and good laws, and so enhance the reputation of the Academy. On the other hand, Euctus and Eulaeus, companions of Perseus, were always complaisant and fell in with his suggestions like his other courtiers. But when he was in flight after his disastrous engagement with the Romans at Pydna, they fell upon him with bitter abuse and reminded him of all his mistakes and oversights, reviling him up and down for every one, until the man was so sick with hurt and anger that he stabbed both of them to death. So much, then, for the limitations of occasion.

But frequently occasions come up unsolicited, and a solicitous friend must not let these slip by but use them. Sometimes a question, a narrative, blame or praise of similar traits in others, provide an opening for outspokenness. An example is the story of Demaratus' arrival at Macedonia at a time when Philip was at odds with his wife and son. Philip welcomed him and asked how the Greeks were faring in the matter of mutual concord. Demaratus, who was on terms of intimacy with him, replied: "A fine thing for you to be asking about concord between Athenians and Peloponnesians when you are indifferent to such a quantity of discord and dissension permeating your own household!" Diogenes too made good use of an opening.

When Philip was on his way to fight the Greeks, Diogenes entered his camp and was brought before him. Philip did not know Diogenes and asked him if he was a spy. "I certainly am, Philip," he said. "I spy on the imprudence and folly which brings you to risk your kingdom and your person in one short throw of the dice." But perhaps this was too extreme.

Another opportunity for admonition offers when people have been upbraided for their failings by others and are abashed and humbled. This situation a tactful man will exploit by silencing the upbraiders and beating them back and then personally taking his friend to task in private and reminding him that he must look out for himself if for no other reason than to thwart his enemies' insolence. "How could those fellows open their mouths, what would they say to you, if you would rid yourself of all this and fling away these invitations to abusive criticism?" The upshot here is that the upbraider will have inflicted a hurt and the admonisher have effected an improvement.

Some people have a neat way of taxing their friends by finding fault with others; they arraign strangers for faults they know their friends are guilty of. Once during an afternoon class my teacher Ammonius noticed that some of the students had had much too elaborate a lunch, whereupon he ordered the freedman to administer a beating to his own servant, remarking, "The fellow can't lunch without vinegar!" At the same time Ammonius looked at us, to include all the guilty in his chiding.

Particular care must be used in reprehending a friend in the presence of others. There is an instructive story involving Plato. Socrates once took one of his acquaintances severely to task in a conversation near the money-changers. Said Plato, "Would it not have been better to say these things in private?" And Socrates, "Would you have not done better to say this to me in private?" Of Pythagoras too it is said that he once inveighed against a pupil too roughly when others were by, and the young man hanged himself; thereafter Pythagoras never admonished anyone when another was by. Admonition of a failing should be like the treatment of an indecent disease or the disclosure of a secret; there ought to be no exhibition or parade to attract witnesses or spectators. It is not the part of a friend but of a performer to seek applause from others' mistakes, to preen oneself before an audience, like surgeons who operate in the theater to get customers. Aside from the affront, which can never be justified in any therapy, consideration must be had for the contentiousness and stubbornness inherent in evil. "A passion reproved," says Euripides, "blows hotter"; but that is not all: if a man is reproved in public and without restraint he will enhance every distemper and every passion to the pitch of shamelessness.

Plato prescribes that elders who seek to implant shamefastness in the young must first themselves be shamefast towards the young: so among friends a bashful outspokenness abashes most effectively. To approach the sinner carefully and tax him without sensationalism is to undermine his sin and wipe it out; showing respect begets respect. The best procedure, then, is to "Bend the head close, that no others may overhear" [*Odyssey* 1.157]. Least of all is it proper to expose a husband in the hearing of his wife, a father in the sight of his children, a lover in the presence of his beloved, or a teacher in the presence of his disciples; pain and anger will drive them distraught if they are chided in the presence of people from whom they expect admiration. It was not so much the wine that exasperated Alexander against Cleitus, in my opinion: it was Cleitus' show of reprimanding him in the presence of other people.

Ptolemy dozed off while receiving an embassy, and his teacher Aristomenes slapped him to wake him up. This gave a handle to the flatterers, who pretended to be indignant on the king's behalf and said, "If with your exhausting labors at all hours you dropped off, we ought to admonish you in private, not lay hands on you before so many people." Ptolemy sent the man a poisoned potion with orders to drink it down. Aristophanes [*Acharnians* 503] declares that Cleon accused him of "Abusing the city when strangers are present" to incite the Athenians against him. This is another failing against which those who wish to use outspokenness, not for display and demagoguery, but to help and heal, must be on guard. Such people should bear in mind what Thucydides represents the Corinthians as saying of themselves—and not a bad saying it is—"We have earned the right to utter reproof." When the Megarian spoke his mind about Greece at the allied council, Lysander said his words needed a country to give them force. Perhaps every man that speaks his mind needs character to give his words force, and most of all when the words are calculated to admonish others and bring them to their senses. Plato used to say that it was by his life that he admonished Speusippus, and Polemon was actually transformed and converted when he saw Xenocrates lecturing and caught a glance from his eye. But when a frivolous and vulgar character sets his hand to outspoken criticism the apt retort is—"Himself blooming with sores he doctors others."

But often circumstances constrain people who are themselves reprehensible to admonish others of their own stripe with whom they are in association. Here the most likely procedure is for the critic somehow to involve himself and include himself in the indictment. Homer provides examples:

> What has happened to us, Diomede, why have we forgotten
> Our strong manhood?

> [*Iliad* 11.313]

and "Hector alone now overmatches us" [*Iliad* 8.234]. This was Socrates' dispassionate way of reproving young men; he did not exempt himself from ignorance but thought he should share with them in the cultivation of virtue and the search for truth. Good will and confidence accrue to men who show that they are subject to the same failings and reform themselves as they do their friends. But a man who takes unction to his own soul as he chastises another, as if he were some lofty being free of passion, does no good and only makes a nuisance and a bore of himself—unless he be of reverend age and possessed of acknowledged dignity and unquestioned reputation. When

he was pleading with Achilles, it was not without design
that Phoenix threw in mention of his own misfortunes,
how he had attempted his father's life in anger and then
quickly repented—"To avoid being called parricide among
the Achaeans" [*Iliad* 9.461]. Phoenix did not wish to seem
sinless and above passion when he was admonishing him.
Such a procedure affects character deeply; men are readier
to yield to others who have undergone similar experience
and do not show contempt.

An inflamed eye should not be exposed to a glaring
light, and neither can a troubled spirit tolerate outspokenness and untempered reproof. A light admixture of praise
makes a useful remedy, as in the following:

> No longer is it seemly for you to be remiss in valor,
> For you are champions in the army. Never would I quarrel
> With any man remiss in fighting because he is a weakling;
> But with you I must remonstrate.

> [*Iliad* 13.116 ff.]

or

> Where are your bow and winged arrows now, Pandarus?
> Where your fame which no man here can match?
> [*Iliad* 5.171 f.]

Men being overborne may very emphatically be recalled
to themselves by such lines as "Where now is Oedipus
and the brilliant riddles?" [Euripides, *Phoenician Women*
1688], or "Can the Heracles who endured so much say
this thing?" [Euripides, *Mad Heracles* 1250].

Not only does such language remit the harsh and peremptory note of censure, but it stimulates a man and
makes him ashamed of bad conduct by reminding him of
good and setting him up as a model for a higher standard.
But if we inject a comparison with other people—his
contemporaries or neighbors or kinsmen—then the contentiousness of wickedness is irritated and flares out and
frequently prompts an angry retort: "Then why don't you
betake yourself to my betters and stop bothering me?"
A man remonstrating with one group must beware of
praising another group—except, by Zeus, parents. Agamemnon, for example, can say to Diomede: "Tydeus be-

got a son very little like him" [*Iliad* 5.800], and Odysseus in the *Scyrians*:

> You shame your illustrious descent; noblest of the Greeks
> Was your father, and you card wool.

For a man who is being admonished to admonish his critic and retort to outspokenness with outspokenness is highly improper. Tempers flare and animosities are created, and the issue would seem to lie not in the give and take of criticism but in inability to accept criticism. It is therefore better to tolerate a friend who thinks he is admonishing you, and then if he subsequently commits a fault and requires admonition this very fact will, as it were, give outspokenness freedom to speak out. If he is reminded, without vindictiveness, that he has himself not been in the habit of overlooking his friends' derelictions but of reproving and informing them, he will yield more readily and accept correction as a requital of good will and courtesy, not of carping and resentment.

"The man who incurs odium for important objects," says Thucydides [2.64], "shows true wisdom." For important objects and where large issues are at stake it is the duty of a friend to incur the odium involved in offering admonition. But if he is peevish at every trifle and confronts his acquaintances not like a friend but like a schoolmaster, then in important matters his admonition will be insipid and ineffective; he will have squandered his outspokenness like a physician who uses up his potent and bitter but essential and expensive drugs on numerous trifling cases where they are not necessary. The critic will himself scrupulously avoid unremittent censoriousness; but if a third person picks at every trifle and keeps up a continual nagging he will have an opening for indicting larger faults. When a man with cirrhosis of the liver brought a sore finger to the physician Philotimus, the doctor said, "Your business, my good sir, is not with a whitlow." So the man who inculpates petty trivialities gives the critical friend an opportunity to say, "Why speak of frolics and drinking and clowning? If this man would only dismiss his mistress or give up dicing he would be an admirable fellow in

every way." If you give a man indulgence for minor pec-
cadilloes he will not resent friendly criticism of greater
faults. A man always on the offensive, everywhere stern
and unsmiling, missing nothing and meddling in everything, is not only a nuisance to his children and his brothers but intolerable to his slaves.

"Not even old age is unqualifiedly bad," says Euripides,
and the same is true of the folly of our friends. We should
therefore keep our friends under surveillance not only
when they are on the mend, and we must begin, by Zeus,
with ready praise. Then, just as iron is softened and made
malleable by heat and then concentrated and given temper
by cooling, so when our friends have been warmed and
made pliant by praise we should apply outspokenness like
a cold dip. We shall then have the opportunity to say,
"Can you reconcile this with that other? Do you see what
advantages goodness bestows? This is what your friends
expect of you, this is your character, this is your natural
bent." But his latter course must be conjured away "To
the mountains or the wash of the thundering sea" [*Iliad*
6.147]. A humane physician would prefer to relieve a patient's malady with sleep and diet rather than castor and
scammony, and so a considerate friend and a good father or
teacher is pleased to use praise rather than blame for
amending character. Far the most effective procedure for
reducing the pain of outspokenness and enhancing its
curative quality is to eschew anger and approach the
sinner with sincere good will. Hence he should not be
sharply disputed when he attempts a denial or silenced
when he makes a defense; we should even somehow help
him frame some creditable excuse. We should ourselves
distrust the worse explanation and suggest a more moderate one, as Hector did to his brother—"Strange man!
It is not fair to keep this wrath in your heart" [*Iliad* 6.326].
Hector presumed that Paris' withdrawal from battle
was not faintheartedness or poltroonery but a fit of temper.
And so Nestor to Agamemnon: "You yielded to your
pride of heart" [*Iliad* 9.109]. I think "your action was unbe-
coming" is more ethical than "your action was wrong," and
"you were careless" than "you were ignorant," and "don't

compete with your brother" than "don't be jealous of your brother," and "keep away from that corrupting woman" than "stop corrupting that woman." This is the mode criticism pursues for purposes of therapy, but for activating its object it follows the opposite mode. When it becomes necessary to sidetrack a man about to take a wrong road, or when we wish to stiffen resistance against some violent drive by proposing a contrary drive, or excite a phlegmatic and listless humor to high achievement, our proper course is to attribute a man's conduct to improbable and discreditable motives. In Sophocles' play, for example, when Odysseus is needling Achilles he says that it is not for the dinner that Achilles is angry, but "In sight of Troy's towers you grow afraid." And when Achilles is indignant at the taunt and speaks of sailing home, Odysseus says:

> I know what you flee—not insult
> But Hector's proximity; staying is not advisable.

By imputing cowardice to a high-spirited and gallant man, licentiousness to a temperate and decent man, niggardliness and avarice to a liberal and generous man, they spur them on to what is noble and divert them from the ignominious. In an irremediable situation they demonstrate their moderation and in their criticism give freer play to sorrow and sympathy than to reproach; but in preventing transgressions and in struggling against passion, they are vehement, inexorable, and indefatigable. This is an occasion for uncompromising good will and undisguised outspokenness.

Even enemies, as we see, chide each other for what they have done. Diogenes used to say that for a man to be saved he needed good friends or flagrant enemies; the former teach, the latter upbraid. But it is better to ward evil off by hearkening to good advice than to repent of evil because of obloquy. It is for this reason that outspokenness requires subtle art; it is the greatest and most potent drug for friendship, but the ingredients must be carefully compounded and the proper juncture for administering it carefully observed.

It is because outspokenness involves pain for the patient, as has been remarked, that we must imitate the practice of physicians. When they operate they do not leave the member affected to ache and smart, but treat it with analgesics and anodynes; nor do dextrous admonishers cast in their mordant sting and then run away. They soothe and refresh with conversation on another subject and with mild discourse, just as stonecutters smooth and polish statues roughhewn and chiseled to shape. If a man is roughhewn and scarred by outspokenness and then left rough and bumpy and uneven, it will be difficult to appeal to him and lull him another time. This is a point to which admonishers should pay particular heed; they ought neither be too quick to leave nor allow an interview to close with remarks calculated to distress and irritate their acquaintances.

Contentment

Peri euthymias, the Greek title of this treatise, is rendered by the Latin *De tranquillitate animi,* and it is therefore generally cited as "On Tranquillity"; "Contentment" is much closer to the Greek. The subject was naturally a favorite with ethical teachers, and we know that Panaetius, Democritus, and others wrote treatises under the same title. Plutarch acknowledges that his own work is a hasty compilation of notes from earlier writings put together hurriedly to be carried to Paccius by their mutual friend Eros, who was on the point of leaving for Rome. We may believe that the work was hurried, for Plutarch does not elsewhere offer the conventional deprecation, but it is nevertheless a well-organized and carefully executed composition. And however much Plutarch may owe to his predecessors, the amiable tone of undoctrinaire edification is surely his own. The treatise is a charming as well as concise epitome of the best ancient thought on the subject, and may be offered as the most attractive specimen and in a sense a summary of Plutarch's ethical essays.

Briefly Plutarch teaches that wealth, distinction, and power can give no contentment unless reason and experience have schooled the soul to make proper use of its blessings and not covet impossibilities. Retirement from active life is a cowardly alternative and must result in betrayal of friends. Blessings must be regarded as transitory and their loss accepted with equanimity. Death must not be feared. Regret, the only emotion against which reason is powerless, can be obviated by consciousness of rectitude. For a man of philosophic temper, the miraculous beauties of the cosmic order make every day a festival.

GREETINGS AND GOOD WISHES, my dear Paccius. It is only a short while since I received your letter urging me to write you a piece on contentment and one on points in Plato's *Timaeus* which require careful exegesis. At the same time it happened that our friend Eros was

obliged to make a trip to Rome; he had received a characteristically peremptory summons from that splendid fellow Fundanus. I hadn't the leisure I would have liked to
comply with your request, and at the same time could not
have a visitor from me call upon you empty-handed, and
so I have put together notes on contentment which I had
made for my own use, in the conviction that what you
desired was not a polished literary composition but something that would be serviceable and helpful. Happily,
though you are on terms of intimacy with great personages
and enjoy an unsurpassed reputation as a public speaker,
you have not fared like Merops in the tragedy, whom
"the admiring crowd made oblivious" to normal reactions.
You bear in mind what you have repeatedly heard, that
gout is not relieved by a fine shoe nor a hangnail by a costly
ring nor migraine by a tiara. How can money or reputation or power at court contribute to serenity of spirit and
untroubled life unless men find their presence agreeable
and do not always miss their absence? And what but
reason can train and habituate us promptly to arrest the
irrational and passionate part of the soul as often as it
rebels and not suffer it to overflow and be swept away because of a momentary situation? Xenophon [*Cyropaedia*
1.6.3] counsels us to be particularly mindful of the gods
and honor them when we prosper so that in time of need
we can call upon them with the assurance that they are
friendly and favorably disposed. It is the same with arguments which are specifics for the passions: sensible people
should rehearse them before the passions arise to have
them in stock for greater effectiveness. Mastiffs bristle at
every voice and are quieted only by the one they are used
to; similarly the passions of the soul are not easily laid
when they grow restive unless there are familiar and firmly
held arguments ready to check their rioting.

"A man who would attain contentment," it has been
said, "must not become involved in business private or
public." In the first place, contentment comes very dear
if its price is inactivity. It is like the advice to the invalid
[in Euripides' *Orestes* 258], "Stay in bed and don't move,
poor fellow"; lethargy is a bad remedy for an ailing frame.

But a psychiatrist does no better if he prescribes sloth and effeminacy and betrayal of friends and relatives and country as a cure for a perturbed and distressed soul. In the second place, it is not true that persons not involved in business are even-tempered. In that case women, whose chief concern is housekeeping, should be more even-tempered than men; but the fact is that though, as Hesiod [*Works and Days* 519] says, the north wind "blows not upon the tender flesh of a maiden," the women's apartment is assailed by more distress and disturbance and depression than you could count because of their jealousy and superstition and ambition and empty notions. Laertes spent twenty years on a farm by himself "with a crone to serve him food and drink" [*Odyssey* 1.191], but though he forsook his country and house and kingship, distress, along with inactivity and depression, kept house with him. Some people idleness reduces to moping, as in this case [*Iliad* 1.488 ff.]:

> But he continued in anger, sitting beside the swift ships,
> The Zeus-descended son of Peleus, swift-footed Achilles.
> Nor ever would he attend the man-honoring assembly
> Nor ever go to war, but wasted his heart, remaining there
> And longed for the battle cry and for war.

Achilles himself avows that it makes him uneasy and fidgety [*Iliad* 18.104]: "Here I sit beside the ships, a useless burden upon the earth." That is why even Epicurus holds that men who are ambitious for distinction should not keep inactive but fulfill their nature by participating in politics and public business; such men are disposed to suffer greater perturbation by reason of inactivity if they fail to reach their goals. But the absurdity of the position lies in urging a public career not on those capable of it, but on those incapable of inactivity. Contentment or its reverse should be defined not by the volume of a man's occupations but by their noble or base quality, for, as has been remarked, the omission of good is no less reprehensible than the commission of evil.

Some specify one particular life, such as the farmer's,

the bachelor's, the king's, as being free of vexation. For such Menander's lines are sufficient admonition:

> I imagined, Phanias, that rich men
> Who need not borrow or groan
> Through the night and toss and turn
> And cry Alack! could sleep sweet
> And soft.

He goes on to observe that rich and poor fare exactly alike:

> Grief must be fused with life.
> It subsists with a luxurious life,
> It attends a famous life,
> It grows old with a needy life.

Timorous and seasick voyagers imagine their plight would be eased if they transferred from a sloop to a merchantman and then from a merchantman to a warship; but their efforts are futile because they carry their bile and their squeamishness with them. So changing one career for another does not relieve the soul of the factors which vex and perturb it—inexperience, unreasonableness, incapacity, and ineptitude in making proper use of what is available. Rich and poor alike are storm-tossed by these factors, they infect the unmarried as well as the married. Because of them men avoid the forum, and then find inactivity intolerable; because of them men seek preferment at court, and when they have attained it find it a burden. "It is being at a loss makes the sick hard to please" [Euripides, *Orestes* 232]; their wives annoy them, they find fault with the doctor, they are dissatisfied with the bed, and "a visitor is a nuisance when he comes and a burden when he goes," as Ion puts it. But when the disease is broken and supplanted by a different condition, access of health makes everything welcome and agreeable; a man who choked on eggs and rusks and crisp rolls yesterday eagerly relishes a coarse loaf with olives and water cress today.

Just such a cheerful change can be introduced into any life by reason. Alexander burst into tears when he heard Anaxarchus speak of an infinity of worlds, and when his friends asked what the matter was, he said: "When worlds are infinite is not our failure to master even one worth crying about?" Yet Crates, with only scrip and poncho, went through life jesting and laughing as if it were a frolic. Agamemnon himself found it troublesome to rule many subjects [*Iliad* 10.88 f.]:

> Agamemnon you must know, Atreus' son, upon whom
> Beyond all men Zeus laid never-ending cares.

But Diogenes sprawled on the block and jeered the auctioneer, and when he ordered him to stand, Diogenes laughed and teased him: "What if you were selling a fish?" Socrates in jail philosophized with his friends; Phaethon mounted to heaven wept because no one would give him his father's horses and chariot. A shoe turns with the foot, not vice versa, and likewise dispositions mold lives to their own fashion. It is not habit, as has been alleged, that makes the best life sweet to those who have chosen it, but it is intelligence which makes a life at once best and sweetest. We should therefore purge the source of contentment which is in ourselves, so that externals also, like familiar things which are our own and which we do not abuse, may profit us.

> It is futile to rail at circumstances
> For they are indifferent. He shall fare well
> Who confronts circumstances aright.

Plato likened life to a game of dice, where we must make an advantageous throw, and then make proper use of whatever falls. The first of these, the advantageous throw, is not in our discretion; but to receive what fate allots properly, to assign each item a place where what we like will do most good and what we dislike least harm —that *is* our function if we are wise. Men who approach life without craftsmanship and intelligence are like sick people who can tolerate neither heat nor cold; prosperity elates them and adversity dejects them. They are perturbed by either lot, or rather by themselves in either lot, and no less in so-called prosperity than in the other. Theodorus called the Atheist used to say that he offered his discourses with his right hand and his hearers received them with the left; the uncultured often show their awkwardness by giving Fortune a left-handed reception when she makes a dextrous presentation. But sensible people behave like bees; bees get honey from thyme, which is very tart and dry, and sensible people often get something appropriate and useful to themselves from the most untoward situation.

This should be the first exercise to practice—like the man who missed the dog with his throw but hit his stepmother: "Not so bad," said he. It *is* possible to divert Fortune from what is unwelcome. Diogenes was banished: "Not so bad"; after he was banished he began to philosophize. Zeno of Citium had one freighter left, and when he heard that it too had foundered with its cargo he remarked, "Well done, Fortune! You have driven me to Stoicism." What prevents us from imitating such models? Your election campaign has miscarried? You shall live in the country and mind your own business. You courted some grandee and were snubbed? You shall be free of jeopardy and distraction. Are you again in some activity which involves time and worry? "Hot water does not so soothe the joints," in the words of Pindar [*Nemean* 4.4], as fame and respect, and a modicum of power makes "Exertion sweet and toil well spent" [Euripides, *Bacchants* 66]. Has malice or envy confronted you with insult and abuse? It is a tail wind that wafts you to the Muses and the Academy, as it was for Plato when Dionysius' friendship broke into a tempest.

This too—the example of famous men who were not affected by adversity—will contribute greatly to contentment. For example, is childlessness a vexation? Consider the kings of Rome, none of whom bequeathed his realm to a son. Are you irked by actual poverty? Is there any Boeotian you would prefer to be rather than Epaminondas, any Roman rather than Fabricius? "But my wife has been seduced." Have you not read the inscription at Delphi, "Placed by Agis, king of sea and land," and have you not heard that Alcibiades seduced Agis' wife Timaia, and that she whispered to her servants that her baby's name was Alcibiades? But this did not prevent Alcibiades from becoming the greatest and most illustrious of the Greeks. Nor did his daughter's debauchery prevent Stilpo from being the most cheerful philosopher of his day. When Metrocles took him to task he said, "Is it my fault or hers?" "Her fault," Metrocles replied, "but your misfortune." "How do you mean?" said Stilpo. "Are not faults slips?" "They are indeed," said Metrocles. "And are not slips debited to those who slip?" Metrocles agreed. "And are not the debits the misfortune of the person debited?" This gentle dialectic demonstrated that the Cynic's scolding was pointless barking.

But most people are irritated and exasperated by the derelictions not only of their friends and relatives but even of their enemies. Upbraiding, irascibility, envy, malevolence, and malignant jealousy pertain only to persons ridden by these pests, and they do burden and exacerbate thoughtless people—neighbors' squabbling, friends' moping, malfeasance of officials in the discharge of their office are examples. I place you high in the list of people bothered by such conduct; like the doctors in Sophocles who "Bitter bile with bitter medicine purge" so you show indignation and exasperation to match their passion and distemper. This is illogical. The business entrusted to your administration is in large part served not by straightforward and upright characters, like tools suited to a job, but by uneven and crooked tools. Do not imagine it is your responsibility to straighten them out, or that it is easy to do. But if you use them for what they are, as a doctor uses dental forceps or surgical clips, and comfort yourself with the calmness and moderation the situation requires, the pleasure you take in your own deportment will be greater than your vexation at the crudeness and depravity of others. You will think that they are only fulfilling their nature, like dogs that bark, and no longer unwillingly concentrate a mass of vexation in a petty and impotent spirit, like scum which flows into a low and hollow sink, and is bound to infect you with others' woes. Some philosophers reprehend even pity bestowed on unfortunates, arguing that to help a neighbor is charity, but that to share his sorrow and surrender to it is not. More than this, when we realize that we are at fault and in a bad state these philosophers forbid us to be disheartened or distressed but enjoin us to apply a proper and objective cure to our malady; consider how unreasonable it is, then, to allow ourselves to be grieved and dejected because not everyone who has business with us or calls on us is an honest gentleman! Take care, my dear Paccius, that our general repugnance to the wickedness we encounter be not an unwitting and timid pretext for love of self, rather than hatred of evil. Vehement concern for politics, and either excessive appetite and pursuit or excessive distaste and revulsion, beget brooding suspicions against men we think deprived us of some things or thrust us into others. The man who has learned to accommodate himself to public business easily and dispassionately turns out to be very affable and gentle in his intercourse with his fellow-men.

But we must revert to our proper subject. In a state of fever anything we taste seems bitter and disagreeable, but when we see others relishing these things without a wry face we no longer blame the food and drink but ourselves and our distemper; so we shall desist from finding fault and being provoked with circumstances if we see others accepting the same conditions calmly and cheerfully. When things fall out not according to our liking it will contribute to our contentment if we bethink us of the agreeable and charming things that are ours; in the mixture the better will eclipse the worse. When our eyes are dazzled by excessive glare we soothe them by turning to green grass and flowers, but our mind we keep intent on what is painful and force it to brood over vexation without respite, all but violently wrenching it from more comforting thoughts. This is an apt context for the remark made to the busybody in the play:

> Why, evil-eyed fellow, look you so keen
> On another's evil and turn a blind eye
> To your own?

Why, my good man, do you stare at your own evil so narrowly and make it vivid and conspicuous, but fail to turn your attention to the good things you have? You concentrate the worst of your qualities against yourself as cupping concentrates the worst humors to draw them out of the body. You are no better than the Chian who sold fine old wine to other people but looked for sour to take with his meal; when one of his slaves asked another what the master was doing when he left, the reply was "Looking for bad when good is available."

The majority do indeed pass by what is potable and good in their own circumstances and rush towards what is troublesome and vexatious. Not so Aristippus; he put the resources he had on the scale, like a good man, and so lightened his woe. He had lost a fine estate, but when a sham friend offered sympathy and condolence he asked the man, "I have three farms left, and you only a plot of ground, I believe?" When his interlocutor agreed, he said, "Then should I not rather condole with you?" To be distressed at what is lost and not rejoice at what is saved is crazy; only a baby will weep and bawl and throw the rest of his toys away if one is taken from him. That is how we behave if, when Fortune has tripped us in one detail, we make all the rest unprofitable by wailing and grieving.

"What do we possess?" a man may ask. What do we not possess? One man has reputation, another a family, another a marriage, another a friend. On his deathbed Antipater of Tarsus made an inventory of the good things that had befallen him, and even included the good trip from Cilicia to Athens. Ordinary things must not be overlooked but taken into account. We ought to be thankful that we are alive and well and see the sun, that there is no war or revolution, that earth and sea lie open for those who wish to till or sail, that we can speak and act or hold our peace and enjoy repose. The presence of these blessings will conduce to our contentment even more if we imagine how it would be if they were not present, if we keep reminding ourselves how the sick yearn for health, men at war for peace, a stranger in the city for friends and reputation, and of how distressing the loss of these things can be. If we do, then we shall not value and cherish these blessings only when we have lost them and depreciate them only when they are safe. Our not having a thing does not raise its value. It is wrong to acquire things in the belief that they are good, to be in constant fear of losing them in the belief that they are good, and yet when we hold them to disregard and despise them as if they were nothing worth. Rather should we use them with pleasure and satisfaction, so that we may easily bear their loss, if that should befall. The majority of men, Arcesilaus remarks, feel obliged to scrutinize other peoples' poems and paintings and statues very carefully, examining each part with mind and eye; but their own lives, which have many features for agreeable contemplation, they overlook. Always they look to other men's reputations and fortunes, as adulterers look to other men's wives, and themselves and their own qualities they despise.

Here is another practice conducive to contentment. It is best, of course, to look to oneself and one's own state, but if not we should contemplate inferiors, and not, as the majority do, compare ourselves with our superiors. Prisoners, for example, regard those released as happy, and these, in turn, freemen, and freemen citizens, and citizens, in turn, the rich, the rich satraps, satraps kings, and kings gods, all but coveting thunder and lightning. Always desiderating what is beyond them, they are never pleased with what they have.

> The wealth of gold-abounding Croesus
>   Is no concern to me;
> Ambition offers no temptation;
>   From envy I am free.
> The gods' affairs I do not question;
>   No monarch would I be.
> I am content, where'er I'm sent
>   With mediocrity.
>   [Archilochus 25, tr. N. H. Dole.]

"A Thasian's sentiment," it will be objected. But there are Chians and Galatians and Bithynians who are dissatisfied with the reputation or power they have got among their countrymen and wail because they cannot sport the patrician badge, and if they can, because they are not praetors, and if they are, because they are not consuls, and if they are, because they were nominated second instead of first. What is this but scraping up excuses for ingratitude to Fortune and penalizing and tormenting oneself? But the sensible man whose thinking is wholesome knows that the sun looks down on untold myriads of men, "As many as enjoy the produce of broad earth" [Simonides], does not sit downhearted and humiliated because there are some more famous and richer than he, but reflects that his life is better and more respectable than millions of others and goes his way singing hallelujahs to his tutelary deity and to his life.

At Olympia you cannot win by choosing your competitors, but the rules of life allow you to vaunt your superiority over many others, to be enviable rather than envious —unless you set yourself up to rival a Briareus or a Heracles. So whenever you admire a man carried in a sedan chair as being superior, stoop to look at the carriers too. And whenever you call Xerxes blessed, as the Hellespontine did when he saw him crossing the bridge, look at the poor devils digging at Athos under the knout and having their ears and noses cut off because the waves broke the bridge down, and reflect on what is in their mind: they call *your* life and *your* state blessed.

When Socrates heard one of his friends complain that the city was dear—"Chian wine a mina, purple cloth three minas, a dram of honey five drachmas"—he took hold of him and brought him to the grain vendors. "Half a peck for an obol—the city is cheap"; then to the oil men— "A quart for two coppers"; then to the clothing merchants—"A gown for ten drachmas—the city is cheap." So when we hear anyone remark that our situation is mean and irksome because we are not consuls or governors, we can say, "Our situation is brilliant, our life enviable: we are not beggars, or porters, or flatterers."

But folly has habituated us to live with a view to others rather than to ourselves, and our nature holds so much envy and malice that our pleasure in our own advantages is not so great as our distress at others'; it behooves you, therefore, to look not merely at the brilliance and fame of those you envy and admire but to roll back the spangled curtain of their reputation, as it were, strip the veneer off and get inside, and behold the many troublesome and disagreeable aspects of their being. The famous Pittacus, whose courage and wisdom and justice were so widely acclaimed, was entertaining guests when his wife came storming in and overturned the table. His guests were embarrassed, but Pittacus said: "Each of us has his trouble; a man with mine is to be congratulated."

> This man the market place counts happy
> Is a heap of misery when he opens his door:
> His wife is emperor and general and always embattled.
> He has much to vex him, I have naught.

Many such vexations, which wealth and fame and royalty entail, are imperceptible to the commonality, for they are benighted in a fog. For his extrinsic pomp, his arms and horses and warrior host, Agamemnon is felicitated as "Atreides, favored by Fortune's weird" [*Iliad* 3.182]; but from within the voice of his own suffering bears witness against this empty glory: "Zeus son of Cronus has bound me fast in heavy doom" [*Iliad* 2.111], and

> I envy you, old man;
> I envy any man who has passed through life
> Without danger, without fame, without glory.
> [Euripides, *Iphigenia at Aulis* 16 ff.]

Such reflections as these will serve to skim off that carping at Fortune which humbles and forfeits our own assets by admiration of our neighbor's.

A very considerable handicap to contentment is our failure to temper our ambition, as a skipper reefs his sails, to the energy available. Our hopes reach out for too much, and when we fail we blame fortune and doom instead of our own folly. It is not bad luck which prevents a man from practicing archery with a plow or hunting rabbits with an ox, it is not a malignant deity which keeps him from catching stag or boar with fishing tackle; to attempt the impossible is stupid and silly. The culprit is self-love, which impels men to crave primacy and victory in everything and to an irrepressible desire to lay hands on everything. Men not only claim the right to be at once rich and learned and strong and good fellows and agreeable companions and friends of kings and governors of a city, but they are dejected if they do not also own blue-ribbon dogs and horses and quails and cocks.

The elder Dionysius was not content with being the greatest dictator of his time, but because he could not rhyme better than the poet Philoxenus or down Plato in dialectic, he flew into a rage and in his exasperation threw Philoxenus into the stone quarries and sent Plato to Aegina to be sold into slavery. Not so Alexander; when the champion Crison seemed to slacken speed on purpose in a race with him he got very angry. When Achilles says [*Iliad* 18.105], "Of the bronze-armed Achaeans none is my peer," he subjoins, "In battle; in council others are better." When Megabyzus the Persian visited Apelles' studio and undertook to babble about art, Apelles shut his mouth with the remark: "So long as you held your peace you seemed to be somebody because of your gold and purple, but now the apprentices grinding the colors are laughing at your foolishness."

When some people hear that the Stoics call their sage not only wise and just and brave but also an orator, poet, general, millionaire, king, they think it funny, and yet they themselves claim all these graces and are irked if they do not get them. But even among the gods each has his own province; one is styled "of war," another "of prophecy," another "of gain," and Zeus assigns Aphrodite to weddings and the bridal chamber "for that she hath no share in deeds of war."

It is in the nature of certain pursuits that they cannot exist side by side but must be in conflict with one another. For example, practicing declamations and studying mathematics require leisure and freedom from distraction, whereas success as a public official or courtier is impossible without preoccupation and activity. Again, "wine and a meat diet render the body stout and robust, but the soul weak." Constant care and vigilance in money matters augments wealth, but a detached disdain of wealth is an effective viaticum for the road to philosophy. Not everything is for everyone; one must heed the Pythian injunction to know himself and then occupy himself as Nature intended and not override her by compulsive emulation of one mode of life after another. [As Pindar says:]

> The horse is for the chariot, the ox for the plow,
> The dolphin swiftly skims the sea at the vessel's side;
> If a man would slay a boar he must find a rugged hound.

Only a lunatic is impatient and vexed because he is not at once a lion "Mountain-ranging, confident in his strength" [*Odyssey* 6.130], and a Maltese lap dog for a widow to pet. Equally silly is the man who would be an Empedocles or Plato or Democritus, writing on the universe and the nature of reality, and at the same time sleep beside an elderly heiress like Euphorion or tipple with Alexander's cronies like Medius, who is indignant and irritated if he is not admired for his wealth like Ismenias and for his courage like Epaminondas. Runners are not downhearted because they do not carry off the wrestler's crown, but take pride and pleasure in their own accomplishment. "Sparta is your portion: cultivate Sparta!" So Solon said:

> We shall not exchange our virtue for their wealth,
> For virtue is stable, whereas money now one has,
> Now another.

When the physicist Strato heard that Menedemus had many more pupils he said: "Is it strange that more people want baths than an athlete's rubdown?" In a letter to Antipater Aristotle writes: "Alexander is not the only one entitled to be proud, because he rules many subjects; those whose speculations on theology are correct also have an equal claim." Men who have so high a regard for their own attainments will not be disturbed by the attainments of their neighbors. We do not expect a vine to bear figs or an olive grapes, but when it comes to ourselves, if we do not possess the combined advantages of millionaire and scholar and general and philosopher, of the flatterer and the plain speaker, of the frugal and the extravagant, we calumniate ourselves and are irked with ourselves and despise ourselves as leading a drab and curtailed life.

There is another lesson, which Nature herself teaches. For diverse beasts she has provided diverse sustenance, and has not made them all flesh-eaters or seed-pickers or root-grubbers; for mankind too she has vouchsafed various avenues to a livelihood—"Shepherd, plowman, fowler, him the sea sustains" [Pindar *Isthmian* 1.48].

Men should choose the calling suited to them, concentrate upon it, and let the others be; they should not take exception to Hesiod's dictum [*Works and Days* 25]: "Potter envies potter, builder builder."

Actually men do not limit their jealousy to fellow-craftsmen and men of their own class, the rich envy the learned, the famous the rich, the lawyers the professors, and freeman and patricians, by Zeus, grow delirious in blessing deft comedians on the stage and ballet dancers and servants in royal courts, thus inflicting no small vexation and unhappiness upon themselves.

Differences in our emotions make it plain that each man holds the cellars of contentment and discontent within himself; the jugs of good things and bad are not deposited "on Zeus' threshold" but in the soul. The foolish overlook and neglect the good things that are there because their imagination is always straining towards the future, but the wise make even things of the past vividly present by recalling them. The present offers itself to our touch for only an instant of time and then eludes the senses; fools think that it is no longers ours, that it no longer pertains to us. There is a painting of a ropemaker in hell with an ass gobbling up all the rope he makes as he plays it out; so the multitude is overtaken and held fast by insensate and ingrate forgetfulness, which erases every deed and every success and every pleasant experience of ease and companionship and enjoyment. It never allows life to grow into a unity, with the past interwoven with the present, but separates yesterday from today as though it were a different substance, and today from tomorrow, as if it were not the same; forgetfulness transforms every occurrence into a non-occurrence. The logic of the schoolmen who deny the principle of growth on the ground that being is in constant flux would continually transform each of us into a different man; so those who do not retain and cherish the past in memory but allow it to flow away, actually make themselves empty and impoverished day by day and dependent upon the morrow, as though all that had occurred yesterday and the day before had not happened at all and had no relevance to them.

If this is one factor that confounds contentment, a greater is when men glide away from what is amiable and easygoing to entangle themselves in memories of disagreeable experiences, like flies that slip off the smooth parts of a mirror and cling to the rough places where there are cracks. Better, like the beetles in Olynthus, which, when they have fallen into a place called Beetles' Doom, cannot get out but twist and turn until they die, so men who have subsided into memory of their misfortunes have no wish to struggle up and breathe free again. We ought to put the bright and attractive in the foreground of our soul, as we do colors in a picture, and de-emphasize or suppress the gloomy; to blot them out or banish them altogether is impossible. "The harmony of the universe is alternately tensed and relaxed, like a lyre or a bow"; and in the affairs of men too nothing is pure and unmixed. In music there are deep notes and shrill, and in grammar vowels and consonants, and the musician or grammarian does not dislike and avoid one or the other but understands how to blend them for his own purpose and use them. In human affairs too there are opposing elements, for as Euripides says:

> Good and bad may not be dissevered;
> There is, as there should be, a commingling.

The one element ought not make us downhearted and despondent; rather like musicians who dull the edge of the bad with the better and swathe the inferior with the good, we ought to make our life a tuneful blend which is appropriate to ourselves.

Menander says,

> Beside each man at his birth there stands a daimon
> To be his good guide through life.

Menander is wrong, and Empedocles has it right: *pairs* of daimones or norns receive each of us at birth and direct us:

> Earth-maiden was there and Sun-maiden who sees afar;
> Bloody Strife and stable Harmony,
> Beauty and Ugliness, Haste and Loitering,
> Charming Infallibility and darkling Dubiety.

At birth we receive the seeds of each of these traits in a mixture, which produces marked unevenness. A sensible man prays for the better but anticipates the other as well, and, avoiding extremes, makes use of both. Epicurus remarks that "the man least dependent upon the morrow goes to meet the morrow most cheerfully"; just so do wealth and reputation and power and preferment give the greatest satisfaction to those least apprehensive of their opposites. A vehement desire for these things begets a vehement fear of their not lasting, and this makes the enjoyment of them unstable, like a flickering flame. But if Reason has equipped a man to say to Fortune, without fear or trepidation, "Very nice, if you bring me something; no harm if you do not," his stoutheartedness, the fact that he does not fear that loss would be intolerable, enables him to enjoy his present blessings with the greatest satisfaction.

Upon the death of his son, Anaxagoras said, "I knew I had begotten a mortal." We may not only admire his composure but imitate it and say, when any adversity befalls, "I know that wealth is transitory and impermanent. I know that those who bestow office can take it away. I know that my wife is good, but a woman, and that my friend is a man, a creature naturally changeable, as Plato says." When unwanted (but not unexpected) accidents befall people who have schooled themselves to such composure there is no place for such protestations as "I would never have thought it. I anticipated something different. I had not expected this." Such composure banishes the leaping and fluttering of the heart and quickly restores its excitement and confusion to stability. In affairs of moment it is solely the element of the unexpected, as Carneades reminds us, that reduces us to distress and despair. The Macedonian kingdom was a tiny fraction of the size of the Roman empire, yet when Perseus lost Macedonia he bewailed his lost most bitterly, and everyone regarded him as the most unfortunate and ill-starred of men. His conqueror Aemilius handed his supreme command by land and sea to his successor, received a wreath and offered sacrifice, and was counted blessed, and rightly. He knew he would relinquish the office he had received, whereas Perseus lost his when he did not expect to. Well has our poet taught us the power of the unexpected: when Odysseus' dog fawned upon him he wept, but when he sat by his tearful wife he showed no such feeling. In the latter case he had come prepared in advance, keeping his emotion under the control of reason, but the former case was a contretemps into which he had fallen suddenly and unexpectedly.

Of unwelcome occurrences, generally speaking, some naturally entail grief and vexation, but in the case of most a false conception has schooled and habituated us to be irked by them. As a specific against the latter it is advisable to keep a line of Menander handy: "Nothing has happened to you unless you make much of it." His meaning is that your body and soul need not be affected if, for example, your father is lowborn, your wife taken in adultery, yourself deprived of some honorary crown or front-seat privilege, for none of these prevents a man from thriving in physique or psyche. For the former category—sickness, hardship, the death of friends or of children—which seem naturally to entail grief and vexation, the line of Euripides should be kept handy: "Alas!—but why Alas? It is the lot of mortality we experience." No logic can so effectively brake the descending spiral of our emotions as the reflection that it is only through the common compulsion of Nature which is an element in his physical constitution, that man is vulnerable to Fortune; in his most essential and greatest aspects he stands secure.

When Demetrius took the Megarians' city he asked Stilpo whether any of his goods had been looted. "I saw no one going off with *my* goods," said Stilpo. When Fortune plunders and confiscates all else we still have within us a thing "such as Achaeans can neither rape nor plunder." It follows that we must not underrate and dismiss Nature as being incapable of prevailing over or even withstanding Fortune. On the contrary, we know that the corruptible and unresisting part of man which is vulnerable to Fortune is small, whereas we ourselves are masters of the better part in which are firmly fixed the greatest of our goods—right opinions and knowledge and reasoning whose consummation is virtue—which can neither be alienated nor destroyed. Undismayed and with hearts courageous we face what is to be and say to Fortune what Socrates said to his judges when he was ostensibly speaking to his accusers: "Anytus and Meletus can kill me, they cannot harm me." Fortune can infect a man with sickness, take his money away, malign him to his countrymen or a tyrant; but she cannot make a good and virile and high-spirited man a poltroon or mean-spirited or ignoble or envious, nor can she rob us of the serenity whose permanent availability is more useful for facing life than a pilot is for facing the sea. No pilot can calm rough wave and wind, or find a haven at will for his need, nor abide what is to be without fear and trepidation. So long as he has not despaired, he uses his skill

> To escape the hellish sea,
> Mainsail lashed at mast's bottom;

but when the sea shows its strength he sits shivering and shaking. But a wise man's serenity affords an expanse of calm to the bodily factors. By self-control and a prudent way of life and moderate exertion, he banishes susceptibility to disease; and if trouble of an outside origin befalls he skims by the reefs "riding a poised and light beam," as Asclepiades says. But if some great and extraordinary calamity overtakes and masters him, then a haven is ready at hand and he can swim from his body as from a boat with seams opened.

It is fear of death, not craving for life, that makes a fool hang on to his body and wind himself about it as Odysseus clung to the fig tree for fear of lurking Charybdis. "The gale suffers him neither to halt nor sail"; he is displeased with what is, and afraid of the alternative. But a man who has attained an understanding of the soul and has calculated that death may be a change for the better, but certainly not for the worse, has in indifference to death no inconsiderable resource for facing life with contentment. A man who can lead an agreeable life when the satisfactory and congenial element is in the ascendant and depart fearlessly when the uncongenial and unnatural assail him and say, "The god will himself release me whensoever I will" [Euripides, *Bacchae* 498], is impregnable to any imaginable difficulty or distemper or agitation. It was not bolts or bars or walls that gave his confidence to the man who said, "I have forestalled you, Fortune; I have blocked your every access to me"; it was by precepts and doctrines which are available to everyone. Utterances of this kind should not be dismissed or distrusted; one should admire and emulate and be inspired by them to put himself to the proof, testing himself in lesser matters as preparation for greater, not evading or thrusting away the care of the soul or taking refuge in the thought that "probably nothing too disagreeable will happen." The luxury-loving soul which is preoccupied with what is easiest and retreats from what it doesn't like to what is most agreeable begets nervelessness and undisciplined effeminacy. But the soul which devotes study and the inexorable force of logic to formulate a detailed conception of what disease and hardship and exile are will find much that is spurious and empty and unsound in things seemingly difficult and formidable. Reason will demonstrate this in every case.

And yet Menander's line—"No man alive can say, This shall not happen to me"—terrifies many people—because they do not realize how much it contributes to serenity to train oneself to be able to look Fortune in the face with eyes wide open and not to foster in oneself fancies dainty and soft, embowered in the shade of many hopes which yield to every pressure and offer resistance to none. We can indeed agree with Menander's "This shall not happen to me," and declare, while we are men alive, "This I shall

not do: I shall not lie, nor cheat, nor defraud, nor con-
spire." This lies within our power, and it is no slight contribution to contentment but a very great one. On the other
hand,

> My conscience, my own awareness
> That I have committed a wrong

leaves behind in the soul, like an ulcer in the flesh, a
trauma which always aches and draws blood. Other pangs
reason can allay, but reason is the very thing that produces
regret; it is the soul and its sense of shame that gnaws and
scourges itself. The shivering and burning caused by ague
or fever are more annoying and distressing than heat or
cold from an outside source; similarly the darts of Fortune
inflict lighter pain for they asail us from without. But the
dirge we keen over offenses that issue from within ourselves—

> None other than I is to blame for these things;
> I myself am guilty—

exacerbates the pain by compounding it with shame.

It follows that no costly mansion, no mass of gold, no
pride of race, no grandeur of office, no charm or force of
eloquence can bestow upon life so clear-skied a serenity
as a soul purged of evil deeds and thoughts which keeps as
the fountain of life a character imperturbable and untainted. From this fountain flow fair deeds which combine
inspired and glad activity carried on with a high heart and
a memory sweeter and solider than that Pindar speaks of
as sustaining old age. "Even when they are emptied," says
Carneades, "censers retain their bouquet for a long while";
and in the soul of a sensible man fair deeds leave behind
a memory always pleasing and always fresh. By this
memory satisfaction in fair deeds is kept watered, so that it
thrives and despises such as bewail life and complain of
it as a domain of evil or a place of exile appointed for
souls in this world.

I like what Diogenes said when he saw his Spartan host
outdoing himself in preparing for a certain festival: "Isn't
every day a festival in the sight of a good man?" And a

very splendid festival if we have good sense. The universe is a temple of the highest holiness and sanctity. Into this temple his birth introduces man as a beholder not of images made by man and incapable of movement but of such as the divine intelligence has revealed as imitations of ideas perceptible to the senses, in Plato's language, with the source of life and movement inherent in them—the sun and the moon and the stars and the rivers which continually send forth new water and the earth which continually sends up sustenance for plants and animals. Life is an initiation and consummation of these mysteries and should therefore be filled with contentment and joy. We should not, like the crowd, wait for such occasions as the Cronia and Diasia and Panathenaea and the like to take pleasure and recreation, purchasing laughter of mimes and dancers for cash payment. We observe the proprieties as we sit there, to be sure, and watch our tongues, for no one complains while he is being initiated or laments while he is attending the Pythia or drinking at the Cronia; but they shame the festivals which the god organizes for us and initiates us into by passing the greater part of their time in complaints and heavyheartedness and crushing anxiety. Men take delight in the sweet strains of instrumental music and in the singing of birds, they take pleasure in the spectacle of animals frisking and frolicking and dislike it when they roar and bellow and scowl. But when they see that their own life is unsmiling and brooding and crushed and ground down by highly disagreeable and unending passions and preoccupations and worries, they find no respite or refreshment for themselves—how could they? Not only so, but when others invite them to do so they will heed no agument whose acceptance would enable them to tolerate the present without recrimination, recall the past with gratitude, and face the future without apprehension or misgivings but with hope glad and shining.

The Mentor Philosophers

THE AGE OF BELIEF: The Medieval Philosophers
selected and edited by Anne Fremantle
The wisdom of a spiritually harmonious age, the 5th
to the 15th Century, embodied in selections from
the basic writings of its important philosophers.
(#MD126—50¢)

THE AGE OF ADVENTURE: The Renaissance Philosophers
selected and edited by Giorgio de Santillana
The basic writings of Da Vinci, Machiavelli, Erasmus,
Montaigne, Copernicus, Kepler, Galileo, and other
great philosophical innovators in an age of adventure
on land and sea and into new realms of thought.
(#MD184—50¢)

THE AGE OF REASON: The 17th Century Philosophers
selected and edited by Stuart Hampshire
Selections from the basic writings of Descartes, Leib-
niz, Spinoza and other great philosophers of "the
century of genius," when science began to influence
philosophical thought. With a penetrating introduction and interpretive commentary. (#MD158—50¢)

THE AGE OF ENLIGHTENMENT: The 18th Century
Philosophers   *selected and edited by Isaiah Berlin*
Basic writings of Berkeley, Locke, Hume and other
brilliant philosophers of the rational and human-
istic age which believed that science's achievements could be translated into philosophical terms.
(#MD172—50¢)

THE AGE OF IDEOLOGY: The 19th Century Philosophers
selected and edited by Henry D. Aiken
The basic writings of Kant, Fichte, Hegel, Schopen-
hauer, Mill, Spencer, Nietzche, Marx and other great
19th century thinkers whose revolutionary ideas led
up to the philosophic dilemmas of our own day.
(#MD185—50¢)

THE AGE OF ANALYSIS: 20th Century Philosophers
selected and edited by Morton White
The philosophy of our day, in all its complexity and
diversity, embodied in the writings of leading 20th
century philosophers, and clearly interpreted by Morton White of the Department of Philosophy, Harvard.
(#MD142—50¢)

The Mentor Religious Classics

THE HOLY BIBLE IN BRIEF *edited and arranged by James Reeves*
The basic story of the Old and New Testaments told as one clear, continuous narrative in the words of the authorized King James text. (#Ms116—50¢)

THE PAPAL ENCYCLICALS in Their Historical Context *edited by Anne Fremantle*
The teachings of the Catholic Church as expressed by the Popes in their official letters. (#MD177—50¢)

THE MEANING OF THE GLORIOUS KORAN. *An explanatory translation by Mohammed Marmaduke Pickthall*
The complete sacred book of Mohammedanism, translated with reverence and scholarship—full historical introduction. (#MD94—50¢)

THE WAY OF LIFE: Tao Tê Ching *by Lao Tzu, translated by R. B. Blakney*
A masterpiece of ancient Chinese wisdom presenting the philosophy of Taoism. (#M129—35¢)

THE SONG OF GOD: BHAGAVAD-GITA *with an Introduction by Aldous Huxley*
The timeless epic of Hindu faith vividly translated for Western readers by Swami Prabhavananda and Christopher Isherwood. (#M103—35¢)

THE SAYINGS OF CONFUCIUS *a new translation by James R. Ware*
The sayings of the greatest wise man of ancient China. (#M151—35¢)

THE TEACHINGS OF THE COMPASSIONATE BUDDHA *edited, with commentary by E. A. Burtt*
The best translations of the basic texts and scriptures, early discourses. The Dhammapada, and later writings of the religion of Buddhism. (#MD131—50¢)

THE UPANISHADS: Breath of the Eternal *translated by Swami Prabhavananda and Frederick Manchester*
Concerned with the knowledge of God and the highest aspects of religious truth, these ancient Hindu scriptures are presented in a readable translation. (#MD194—50¢)

MENTOR Books of Special Interest

MYTHOLOGY

Edith Hamilton. A brilliant presentation of the classic Greek, Roman and Norse legends. By the author of *The Greek Way.* (#MD86—50¢)

GODS, HEROES AND MEN of Ancient Greece

W. H. D. Rouse. The distinguished translator of the Mentor *Iliad* and *Odyssey* re-tells the ancient Greek legends in a lively, informal narrative for readers of all ages. (#Signet Key Ks353—35¢)

GREEK HISTORICAL THOUGHT

Edited by Arnold J. Toynbee. The eminent historian's outstanding translations of Greek historical experience from Homer to the age of Heraclius —a stimulating guide for our own times. (#MD164—50¢)

THE ILIAD OF HOMER

Translated by W. H. D. Rouse. A spirited prose translation of Homer's epic about the Trojan War by a noted English scholar. (#MD110—50¢)

THE ODYSSEY

Translated by W. H. D. Rouse. A modern prose translation of the world's greatest adventure story, the travels of Ulysses. (#MD92—50¢)

EIGHT GREAT TRAGEDIES

Edited by Sylvan Barnet, Morton Berman, and William Burto. The world's great dramatic literature, eight memorable tragedies by Aeschylus, Euripides, Sophocles, Shakespeare, Ibsen, Strindberg, Yeats, and O'Neill. With essays on tragedy by Aristotle, Emerson, and others. (#MD195—50¢)

AMERICAN ESSAYS (expanded)

Edited by Charles B. Shaw. A lively sampling of American thought from the 18th century to present: 34 superb essays by Franklin, Mencken, Lippmann, and others. (#MD137—50¢)

THE WORLD OF HISTORY

Advisory editors: Crane Brinton, Alfred Kazin and John D. Hicks. An engrossing journey through the living past, this exciting selection of the best in contemporary historical writing makes history meaningful and vivid for the reader of today. With an introduction by Allan Nevins. (#M109—35¢)

HISTORY OF THE WORLD IN 240 PAGES

René Sédillot. Complete in one volume, the whole story of world history from prehistoric times to the present. Fascinating, authoritative, ideal for rapid reference. (#MD88—50¢)

ADVENTURES OF IDEAS

Alfred North Whitehead. By one of the most renowned philosophers of our time, an absorbing account of mankind's great thoughts, which traces the development of crucial ideas from ancient times to the present. (#MD141—50¢)

THE GOLDEN TREASURY

F. T. Palgrave. Enlarged and up-dated by Oscar Williams. Great lyric poems of the English language from 1526 to the present—642 great poems, both classic and modern, by 193 poets. (#MD90—50¢)

Other MENTOR Books You Will Enjoy

Literature and the Arts

THE CREATIVE PROCESS

Edited, with introduction, by Brewster Ghiselin. Thirty-eight of the greatest minds in the world reveal how they actually begin and complete creative work in many fields. (#MD132—50¢)

BOOKS THAT CHANGED THE WORLD

Robert B. Downs. The fascinating histories of sixteen great books—from Machiavelli's *The Prince* to Einstein's *Theories of Relativity*—that have changed the course of history. (#M168—35¢)

GOOD READING (enlarged, up-to-date edition)

Edited by the Committee on College Reading. A carefully selected guide to 1500 useful and entertaining volumes which will help you select your own reading program from the wealth of the world's important literature. Includes checklist of best paperbound titles. (#MD178—50¢)

THE CYCLE OF AMERICAN LITERATURE

Robert E. Spiller. A coherent and striking history of America's literary achievements, by a noted authority. "Stimulating, exciting, and rewarding."—*Boston Herald* (#MD188—50¢)

THE READER'S COMPANION TO WORLD LITERATURE

This alphabetically arranged and comprehensive reference book to the great literature of all ages, answers questions on authors, titles, literary movements and periods, and defines technical terms and phrases. (#MD179—50¢)

The Classics

THE INFERNO BY DANTE

Translated by John Ciardi. One of the world's great poetic masterpieces in a new verse translation in modern English by a celebrated poet. (#MD113—50¢)

THE PRINCE

Niccolo Machiavelli, with an introduction by Christian Gauss. The classic work on statesmanship and power, revealing, in advice to a Renaissance prince, the techniques and strategy of gaining and keeping political control. (#M69—35¢)

LEAVES OF GRASS

Walt Whitman. A complete edition of the incomparable poems of America's remarkable poet, thinker, visionary and exuberant lover of his nation. (#Ms117—50¢)

WALDEN and the Famous Essay on Civil Disobedience

Henry David Thoreau. An American classic, by a rebel against civilization; includes his advice on passive resistance. (#MD176—50¢)

TO OUR READERS: We welcome your comments about Signet, Signet Key and Mentor books. If your dealer does not have the books you want, you may order them by mail enclosing the list price plus 5¢ a copy to cover mailing costs. Send for our free catalog. The New American Library of World Literature, Inc., 501 Madison Ave., N. Y. 22, N. Y.